BUTTERFLY
MESSENGERS

LLOYD HOLLETT

BUTTERFLY MESSENGERS

True Stories of Comfort and Hope

FLANKER PRESS LTD.

ST. JOHN'S

2010

Library and Archives Canada Cataloguing in Publication

Hollett, Lloyd, 1958-
  Butterfly messengers : true stories of comfort and hope / Lloyd Hollett.

ISBN 978-1-897317-77-8

  1. Butterflies--Religious aspects. 2. Human-animal relationships--Religious
aspects. 3. Bereavement--Religious aspects. I. Title.

BL439.H64 2010   202'.12   C2010-902997-6

© 2010 by Lloyd Hollett

PRINTED IN CANADA

MIX
Paper from
responsible sources
FSC
www.fsc.org FSC® C016245

This paper has been certified to meet the environmental and social standards of the Forest Stewardship Council® (FSC®) and comes from responsibly managed forests, and verified recycled sources.

FLANKER PRESS
P.O. BOX 2522, STATION C
ST. JOHN'S, NL A1C 6K1 CANADA
TOLL-FREE: 1-866-739-4420
WWW.FLANKERPRESS.COM

Cover Design: Adam Freake

9 8 7 6 5 4 3 2

  Canada Council Conseil des Arts
for the Arts du Canada   Newfoundland Labrador

We acknowledge the financial support of the Government of Canada through the Book Publishing Industry Development Program (BPIDP) and the Government of Newfoundland and Labrador, Department of Tourism, Culture and Recreation. We acknowledge the support of the Canada Council for the Arts, which last year invested $157 million to bring the arts to Canadians throughout the country. Nous remercions le Conseil des arts du Canada de son soutien. L'an dernier, le Conseil a investi 157 millions de dollars pour mettre de l'art dans la vie des Canadiennes et des Canadiens de tout le pays.

To my parents, Herbert and Effie Hollett

The man whispered,
"God, speak to me."
And a meadowlark sang.
But, the man did not hear.

So the man yelled,
"God, speak to me!"
And the thunder rolled across the sky.
But, the man did not listen.

The man looked around and said,
"God, let me see you."
And a star shone brightly.
But, the man did not notice.

The man shouted,
"God, show me a miracle!"
And a life was born.
But, the man did not see.

So, the man cried out in despair,
"Touch me God, and let me know you are here!"
Whereupon, God reached down and touched the man . . .

But, the man brushed the butterfly away and walked on.

Anonymous

Contents

Preface

Butterflies have intrigued me since my days in college. We had a wonderful instructor, Bill Parrott, who taught a course in Forest Entomology. Entomology is the term for the study of insects. We were given the option of making an insect collection as part of our course, and I was one of only a half-dozen students who chose to do so. It was through Mr. Parrott that I was "bitten by the bug," as I like to say, and I have been collecting ever since. I feel blessed to have been able to turn my passion for butter-flies into a career that is still active after thirty years.

Soon after graduating from college, I was hired by the Provincial Department of Forestry in St. John's, Newfoundland. I spent twenty great years with the department, most of which were spent at Corner Brook, after our headquarters was transferred there in 1984. During my career with forestry, I started an insect col-lection for the department. Some of the insects in this collection were used to prepare displays for each of the forestry unit offices throughout the province. These were on display for school visits to the offices and for when the forestry technicians were invited into the schools for classroom presentations. I also put together a more extensive collection which I used on my many school visits throughout Newfoundland and Labrador.

In the early 1990s I became aware of a facility that was opening in Montreal, Quebec, called the Montreal

Insectarium. After some searching, I was able to make contact with the founder of the Insectarium, Georges Brossard. I sent Georges a request, asking him for some insect specimens to enhance my school presentations. The response I received was quite unexpected—an eight-page handwritten letter, in which Georges suggested that I build an Insectarium in Newfoundland.

My co-worker, Gary Holloway, and I were intrigued by the idea but thought it was too ambitious of a project for a couple of civil servants. After six months of putting the idea on the back burner, however, we decided to give it more serious consideration. It was a long journey and we encountered many obstacles and setbacks, but eight years later we finally saw the realization of our goals when we opened the Newfoundland Insectarium in the fall of 1998.

For those unfamiliar with the term Insectarium, Georges Brossard likes to define it as "a temple dedicated to the most successful animals on earth—the insects." I like to define it as an insect zoo and museum all rolled into one. In addition to thousands of mounted butterflies, beetles, and other insects, there are live displays of ants, bees, tarantulas, and many others. We were very lucky in finding an old dairy barn in the town of Reidville, near Deer Lake, that had been built in the 1940s. It needed a great deal of work, but the three-storey structure that is now the Insectarium boasts a unique architecture to house the series of displays that define the facility.

The specimens needed to fill the Insectarium come from all over the world. Georges Brossard donated thousands of insects from his own private collection.

The rest were sent to us by Natural History museums, universities, and private collectors in nearly 100 countries. We corresponded with over 500 of these facilities and received a great response to our suggestion of trading insects from Newfoundland for insects from their countries. The resulting collection became the basis for the Newfoundland Insectarium.

It became an instant attraction with locals and visiting tourists. Schoolchildren visited for field trips and families bought yearly memberships. It has since become one of the top tourist destinations in Eastern Canada and has welcomed over 200,000 visitors.

In 2002, we added the butterfly pavilion to the Insectarium, which is home to hundreds of free-flying tropical butterflies. We have always felt that the Insectarium was incomplete without live butterflies, so we secured the additional financing and erected a large greenhouse. Butterflies were imported from faraway places such as Costa Rica and the Philippines, and this live exhibition soon became an added bonus for our visitors. It features a pond and waterfall, beautiful plants and flowers, and hundreds of butterflies. Visitors have described the butterfly garden as "like walking in Paradise" and "visiting Heaven."

The addition of the butterfly garden led me to meet many people who have had special encounters with butterflies, stories that always involved a beautiful butterfly and the passing of a loved one. I wish now that I had taken the time to record many of the stories that were told to me. When my mother passed away, I ended up with my own special Butterfly Messenger story, one I will share with you in this book.

After hearing so many people describe their encounters with "spiritual" butterflies, and having had my own experience, I decided to put the stories together in a compilation. This book is a result of this effort and is a collection of stories from throughout Canada and the United States, with the majority coming from Newfoundland and Labrador. The fact that most are from this province is only a reflection of my limited ability to get the word out that I was looking for stories. It does not mean that there are more Butterfly Messenger stories in this province than in other areas. I am sure that there are enough stories out there to fill dozens of books.

To the best of my knowledge, these stories are all true, and they happened directly to the people who wrote them. The authors come from all walks of life and reflect many writing styles and abilities. In my effort to bring some continuity to the book, I have had to do some minor editing with a number of the stories. I have tried not to change the meaning of what the author was trying to express and I have kept each story as original as possible. Several of the longer stories were shortened so that they could be included here. The large number of stories I received made it impossible to include them all. I would like to thank everyone who submitted their Butterfly Messenger stories.

The majority of the stories involve an encounter with a live butterfly after someone close to the person had died. As you will see, however, not all of the stories fit into this category. Butterfly messengers can come in many different forms; you just have to have an open mind to recognize them.

The most touching stories for me were the ones involving children. Parents who have lost a child are often inconsolable in their grief. A visit by a butterfly can sometimes bring a sense of peace and comfort. I am grateful to those parents who took the time to write their stories, as it surely must have brought back painful memories of their loss.

The role of the butterfly varies greatly from story to story. Sometimes the butterfly is a very minor player, appearing briefly at a funeral service or during some special time such as a birthday or anniversary, and then disappearing as quickly as it came. Other times the butterfly is the central player, and the encounter that the person has can only be described as a "miracle." Whether these butterflies are sent by others or whether they just happen to show up when someone desperately needs a "sign," we will never know. I will leave it to the reader to form his or her own opinion. Are they just butterflies out for their daily flight, or are they truly Butterfly Messengers, sent by our loved ones, to reassure us that they are still part of our lives?

Once again, a sincere thank you to all the people who took the time to write their stories. Many of you expressed your desire to help bring a sense of comfort and hope to others by having your stories told. It has been a pleasure and an honour for me to meet many of you through your stories and to share a small part of what, to you, must be a very personal experience.

I would also like to thank you, the reader, for taking the time to experience these stories. I hope you will enjoy reading them as much as I have enjoyed bringing them to you.

Butterflies and Moths

Butterflies and moths are known scientifically as *Lepidoptera*, a Latin word meaning "scaly wings." This is one of the main characteristics of this group of insects, and it distinguishes them from all other types. Their wings are actually covered with thousands of tiny, overlapping scales. These scales are quite often brilliantly coloured, and this results in the wonderful patterns that can be found in both butterflies and moths.

Throughout the world there are approximately 170,000 species of *Lepidoptera*, with about one-tenth, or 17,000 species being butterflies, and the rest moths. In Newfoundland and Labrador, there are approximately sixty-three species of butterflies, with forty-seven species found on the island. There are hundreds of species of moths.

Generally, butterflies and moths have a number of characteristics common to all insects. They have a pair of antennae, four wings, six legs, and three main parts to the body: the head, thorax, and abdomen. In addition to the scaly wings, making them different from other insect types, they also have a unique mouth. The mouth is basically a long, hollow feeding tube, the proboscis, which they keep coiled up beneath the head when not in use. When feeding, they uncurl this tongue and use it much like a person using a straw. The various species have different lengths of tongue, based on the type of flower on which they feed. It should be noted that, because of their unusual mouths, butterflies and moths do not bite and are completely harmless.

As adults, butterflies are only able to feed on fluids. Flower nectar is the major source of sustenance for most species. Other butterfly foods include tree sap, overripe fruit, and liquids found on dung and carrion. Of course, they also drink water, and one interesting behaviour of some species, especially Swallowtails, is to do what's known as "mud puddling." They sometimes gather by the hundreds in moist areas to obtain vital minerals from wet sand and mud.

Although the vast majority of stories in this book are about butterflies, there are several that are about moths. I have often heard small moths referred to as "baby butterflies"; many people have a hard time telling the two apart. There are several main differences between the two groups that make up the *Lepidoptera*. Butterflies have long, thin antennae with a slight club at the tip, while moths have anything from fuzzy to thin antennae, but never with a club at the tip. Butterflies fly during the day while moths generally fly at night. There are, however, a few daytime flying moths. As a general rule, butterflies tend to close their wings when resting, while moths tend to keep them open. Butterflies are usually more colourful than moths, and moths tend to have a larger, thicker body. While each group has its distinguishing characteristics, there are always exceptions to the rule.

Butterflies and moths are from a group of insects that undergo complete metamorphosis. This means that they go through four distinct phases in their development. First there is the egg, then the caterpillar, then the pupa, or chrysalis, and finally, the adult butterfly or moth. The caterpillar is the main growth phase. In order to grow, the caterpillar must shed its skin several times. During the chrysalis stage, the body components of the caterpillar are broken down and reformed into an adult butterfly or moth. This last phase is what has given butterflies such a close association with death and rebirth in humans. The butterfly goes from a cumbersome, earthbound caterpillar to a beautiful butterfly, free to fly up into the heavens.

There are about a half-dozen butterfly species that make up the vast majority of these stories. The butterfly we encounter most frequently is the Monarch. This butterfly is possibly the most recognized butterfly in North America, with its distinct orange and black markings. The most remarkable thing about the Monarch is its migration, which takes it from Canada all the way to the mountains of Mexico and coastal regions of California.

The second group is the Swallowtail. In Newfoundland, the Tiger Swallowtail is the most common, and the one found most in these stories. The Short-Tailed Swallowtail is also mentioned. The other common species are the Red Admiral and the Mourning Cloak.

Then there are the stories about "white butterflies" (Cabbage White), yellow butterflies (Sulfurs), and several others that describe various colours that could be any number of species. Occasionally we hear of a "black and white butterfly" which could refer to the White Admiral. It should be noted that many residents of Newfoundland often refer to the Tiger Swallowtail as a Monarch.

Monarchs, in reality, are very infrequent visitors to the island of Newfoundland and are not seen every year. They do not breed here due to the absence of milkweed, the larval host plant. The only Monarchs found here get blown in from the maritime provinces.

The moth found most frequently mentioned in the stories is the Cecropia Moth. It is one of the biggest moths in North America, and one of the most beautiful. It is common in most parts of the country but very rare in Newfoundland.

The Symbolism of the Butterfly

The "miracle" of a butterfly's transformation from earthbound caterpillar to a beautiful butterfly is certainly symbolic to our religious view of death and our rebirth in spiritual form. For hundreds of years, butterflies have been viewed as a symbol of the human soul by many cultures around the world. The ancient Greeks believed that a new soul was born each time a butterfly emerged from its chrysalis. Early Europeans believed that the human soul took the form of a butterfly. Native American Indian legends told that butterflies would carry the wishes of the Great Spirit into Heaven, there to be granted. The Mayan Indians of Central America looked upon butterflies as the spirits of dead warriors, in disguise and descending from Heaven. The Aztecs of South America believed that spirits, in the form of beautiful butterflies, would visit their relatives to assure them that they were happy and well in their new spiritual world. This belief is very close to our own view of Butterfly Messengers.

For many people, a butterfly is emblematic of transformation, beauty, and peace. What better symbol to be used by someone who has "passed over," than to send a Butterfly Messenger to grieving relatives?

I have heard many stories from those who have lost a loved one, describing their agony over the need to know that their child, parent, or friend is at peace and still around in spiritual form. They often ask for some kind of sign to let them know that there is life after death. They ask that a pencil, or some other object, be moved or manipulated in some way. It very rarely happens. But when they ask to see a butterfly as a sign, they often get rewarded in unexpected and sometimes miraculous ways.

I do not believe that the butterfly is the soul of a loved one. I believe that if we have the ability to move things after we have departed this world, in order to communicate with grieving relatives and friends, one of the easiest things to manipulate would be a butter-fly. They float around effortlessly and seem to be almost weightless. Because of this, and their association with rebirth, I truly feel that they are often used by our loved ones to send us a message. The message is that, although they are no longer with us physically, they are still part of our lives.

These butterflies give us some reassurance that those who have passed on before us are still close by and watching over us. They offer help to reinforce our memories and sense of well-being. Sometimes, if we open our minds and senses, we realize that they are truly Butterfly Messengers.

My Story

LLOYD HOLLETT

When the telephone rang that April morning, I wasn't expecting to hear my sister on the other end of the line. "I have some bad news," she said. "Mom passed away this morning." Although the news was difficult to hear, it was not unexpected. Mom had been suffering the ravages of Alzheimer's disease for a number of years and had been in poor health for quite some time. The shock came from the fact that her death came so soon after our father had passed away, which was only three weeks earlier. I was soon on my way to Fort McMurray, Alberta, to say goodbye once again.

Mom and Dad were from the small community of Little Harbour East in Placentia Bay, Newfoundland. They moved there from the town of Harbour Buffett on Long Island in the early 1960s, before the resettlement program started. Dad was a fisherman and carpenter, and he moved from the islands so that he could work at the carpentry trade during times when the fishery was not so good. Throughout my entire childhood he alternated from carpentry work in St. John's to fishing out of Little Harbour. As a young woman, Mom worked for the merchants of Harbour Buffett but dedicated her time as a homemaker after the move to Little Harbour, raising three children and looking after "her Herbert."

We started to suspect something was wrong when she wouldn't talk on the phone when we called. If she answered she would always pass the phone to Dad right away. She was trying to disguise the fact that she couldn't remember what we said to her. Dad was keenly aware of what was happening and had to adjust his life to enhance hers. No more trips out in the boat for a few cod, as he couldn't leave her alone for that long. He loved when we came for a visit so he and I could go fishing while my wife, Sandy, stayed with Mom.

Over the years, as Mom's condition got progressively worse, it became more difficult for Dad to care for her. In his late seventies, Dad was starting to slow down himself. The option of going into a long-term care facility in Newfoundland was discussed but, because of Mom's condition, they would have to go to different homes which were miles apart. Dad would not hear of being separated from his beloved Effie, so the decision was made for them to move to Fort McMurray, where they could live with my sister Helen. My Dad was now 80 and the move was very painful for him because he loved the salt water and would certainly miss living near the ocean. In addition, Dad's only surviving sibling, his sister Viola, and her husband, Frank, were living in Little Harbour. Uncle Frank was my father's best friend, and Dad knew he would probably not get to see either of them again.

After several years in Alberta, with Dad now in a wheelchair and Mom's illness progressing, they both were at the stage where they needed professional care. Luckily, they were able to go to the same facility, located on the fourth floor of the Fort McMurray Hospital.

Although they would have to have separate rooms, Dad could spend as much time as he wanted with Mom. He would sit in his wheelchair and the staff would wheel Mom over beside him and he would spend hours just holding her hand. During her last year, she lost her ability to talk, but I am sure they were still communicating in their own way.

Once a year, Sandy and I would travel to Alberta to see them. It was difficult to see Mom's condition deteriorating more and more each time we went, especially when she finally could no longer recognize us. We got word in March that Dad was very ill. My sister called to say that we should come right away, so we both flew out to be with him.

We arrived in time for him to recognize us and wonder why we had gone to the expense of coming all that way to Alberta just to see him. That was typical of my father, wondering why we were always fussing over him. He slipped into a coma that same night and never regained consciousness. He lingered near death for four long days while, night and day, we kept vigil by his side.

Each day we would go to Mom's room, put her in the special chair she used, and wheel her down to Dad's room so that we could have them both there together with us. On the day Dad died, several unusual things happened. That afternoon we were all in the hospital room. Mom was sitting quietly in her chair when, in a very clear voice she said, "Go on, go on home." This was the first thing she had said in more than a year, and we were all shocked. It was as if she and Dad were communicating with each other, even though Dad was in a coma and near death and she was in the very advanced stages of Alzheimer's disease. Dad would never do anything unless he had Mom's blessing, so we believe that Mom was telling him that it was okay to let go. He died a few hours later.

A short time after he died, my brother-in-law Keith went to the nurse's station to call the minister to let him know that Dad had passed away. There was nobody there at the time but, as he was standing there, he felt someone give him a big hug. It shook him up so much that he had to sit down for a while. Keith was very close to Dad and did everything for him. I think Dad was letting Keith know how much he appreciated all he had done for him.

Dad asked to be buried in Fort McMurray, instead of being brought back to Newfoundland. His philosophy was, "I can get to Heaven just as easily from here as I can from Newfoundland, so don't go to the expense of shipping me all the way back home." Sandy and I flew back to Newfoundland the day after the funeral. It was very hard to say goodbye to Mom because she was so frail and we knew her time with us might not be long. We didn't realize how little time she had.

So now, here I was preparing to fly back to Alberta for another funeral. This time I went alone, due to the expenses we had just incurred in flying out to be with my father. My two sisters, Linda and Helen, picked me up at the airport in Fort McMurray. It was about 7:30 p.m. on that cold April evening. "Mom is at the church," one of them said. "We can stop in and spend a little time with her before we go back to the house. The visitation for everyone else is tomorrow."

We arrived at the church shortly before dark. As

we climbed the stairs to enter the building, a smile came to my face. I told my sisters to look at the handle of the church door. There, sitting on the handle, was a beautiful butterfly. I said, "Thanks for letting me know that you are still with us, Mom." That butterfly was my sign that she was still around and wanted to let me know that dying is not the end, just a new beginning. We had to encourage the butterfly to move from the handle in order to open the door. We then went inside to spend some time with her. The rest of my time there is just a blur, but I will never forget the Butterfly Messenger that gave us so much comfort in our time of sorrow.

Comfort and Hope

GWEN ANTLE

Marystown, Newfoundland

My precious 22-year-old daughter, Lyndsey, was attending Memorial University in St. John's, working toward a degree in social work. She would have graduated in May 2006, but unfortunately that day would never come. She completed the semester in April of 2005 and returned home for several months. On the weekends, she sometimes went back to St. John's to spend time with her friends. She did this on Friday, June 17, and was planning to return home on Sunday, June 19, for Father's Day. However, at 1:05 a.m. on June 19, while crossing the street in front of City Hall, a taxi struck Lyndsey and her friend. Lyndsey bore the brunt of the collision and suffered multiple skull fractures. She was pronounced brain-dead on June 22 at the Health Sciences Centre. Knowing that she would want it, we donated her organs, and in doing so, she helped to save four lives.

After leaving the hospital in St. John's, we had a three-hour drive home to Marystown, so it was late that night when we arrived at the funeral home to make the arrangements for Lyndsey's funeral. We decided that our family and closest friends would meet at the funeral home at 2:00 p.m. the following afternoon for her wake.

I had no idea how I was going to find the strength

to go inside that funeral home and see my precious baby there. The closer we got, the more desperate I was feeling. When we arrived, 15 minutes late after being slowed down by Lyndsey's sister, Courtney, my brother, Dominic, came up to the car and said, "You have to come over here with us before you go in." I could not imagine what could be so important, but we walked over to where they were all standing.

LYNDSEY ANTLE

Leann, one of Lyndsey's closest friends, handed me a little stuffed bear, and pinned to it was a poem and butterfly brooch. She told me that Lyndsey had given her the teddy bear for Christmas that year and her mom had given her the poem and brooch the day before to comfort her. She had planned to put the bear in the coffin with Lyndsey, but had wanted me to read the poem. The verse read:

"Till We Meet Again" Angel:

"Even though we must be apart, know that when you
hear the whisper of the wind, it will be me saying hello;
when you smell the first fragrant flowers of spring, you
will feel my presence; and when you see a butterfly, you
will know I have just passed by; and this thoughtful little angel will remind you how very much I care for you;
and I want you to wear it till we meet again!"

I read the poem and, although it was comforting, I
was so overwhelmed with despair and shock, nothing
was really registering. Leann wanted me to keep the
poem and brooch, which I greatly appreciated. Then
Lyndsey's other friend and roommate, Ashley, said, "And
here is the butterfly!" She held out her two hands, and
there in the centre of her palms was a huge black butterfly. It was just sitting there on her hands. They then told
us that the butterfly had landed at Robert's feet (Robert
is the father of Lyndsey's high-school sweetheart) about
15 minutes before we arrived. He put his hand down and
the butterfly crawled onto his hand. It stayed there until
Ashley put her hands out, and it crawled from his hands
to hers. When I saw it, I felt a need to stroke its wings. It
stayed there on her hands and let me stroke its wings
three times before it flew away. Then my sister Barb said,
"Gwen, look at all the girls." She and all of Lyndsey's
friends were wearing butterfly necklaces. The beautiful
butterfly had arrived 15 minutes earlier, which is the time
we were scheduled to be there.

The arrival of the butterfly helped our family and I,
and Lyndsey's friends, face going inside to see her that

day. It truly felt like she was letting us know she still lived on and that her passing was not the end. It gave us hope.

There was a fundraiser held in Lyndsey's name, and all of her friends painted small butterflies on their cheeks in honour of her. I now know that the butterfly was a Black Swallowtail.* I had never seen that type of butterfly before or since her wake.

When remembering the time we spent at the hospital, waiting and praying for Lyndsey to recover from the coma, I remember that every time I went outside to be by myself to pray, cry and get some air, there was always one or several big yellow butterflies with me. Also, during the three-hour drive home from the hospital after Lyndsey passed, Courtney wanted something to drink, so while we waited for her, I got out of the car to have a cigarette. Once again, there was a big yellow butterfly circling my legs the whole time we were there. I also know now that the yellow butterfly was a Tiger Swallowtail.

The funeral director, Lorraine Blunden, told me that even though she had never met Lyndsey or our family before, she grew to love her from hearing about the kind of person she was from her friends and family. She wanted to do something special for Lyndsey and for us, and secretly asked my nieces to help her with this. They made beautiful, colourful, butterfly pins and Lorraine presented them to us on the day of Lyndsey's funeral to wear in memory of her. We all thought it was such a beautiful and caring thing for her to do—but there was more to come.

Several weeks later, we brought her belongings

home from her apartment in St. John's. This was something I could not bear to face. I had moved her to and from St. John's so often for university, and then home again for the summer, and I could not face bringing her things home for the last time, so her best friend, Daisy, my brother Dominic, and my partner, Leo, offered to take on the difficult task.

One of the first things I unpacked was a valance she used on her window. It was just a plain piece of pink cotton with shower curtain rings pushed through the material to hang on the rod. What amazed me was that between every second ring she had pinned a butterfly to the material. Even though I had seen the valance in her room, I had never noticed this. The butterflies she used were the exact same butterflies that Lorraine had used for our pins the day of her funeral, which, of course, Lorraine had no way of knowing.

When my sister Barb returned to work in Corner Brook after Lyndsey's funeral, her friend, Nancy, gave her a little gift. She explained to Barb that she felt that she had to do this for her. To Barb's amazement, her friend presented her with the exact same poem and brooch that Leann had given me, "Till We Meet Again!" Nancy had had no way of knowing anything about our amazing butterfly experience, yet she chose the exact same gift.

Several months later, while again going through Lyndsey's things, I found a poster she had made for one of her social work projects. She had drawn a cater-pillar, cocoon, and butterfly using the butterfly's life-cycle stages to demonstrate the various stages of development in social work. I didn't remember her doing this, but Courtney did. I felt that all of the butterfly experiences were signs and messages from Lyndsey, but when I saw the poster, it confirmed without a doubt that she had used that Black Swallowtail butterfly on the day of her wake to let us know that, although she was physically gone, her energy was still with us in a different form and that she lived on, just as a caterpillar is not here physically anymore after it transforms into a beautiful butterfly, but it is still part of the butterfly.

I guess we all think butterflies are beautiful, but I do not think that this is the only reason she sends her messages through them; I feel it was the symbolism that she is trying to convey to us. Her poster proved that to me because she had already used a butterfly as a symbolism for social work, so I know it meant more to her than just something pretty to look at. I realize now that she knew that I and everyone else who cared about her would get it. And we did.

Since then, she has sent us more signs using butterflies. For example, each year, just before Christmas, usually between the twelfth of December and Christmas Eve, one of my butterfly suncatchers falls off the window. It has not failed yet. Lyndsey loved Christmas.

I do not want to make anything into something it is not, and I don't believe it is just for the sake of believing, but there have been so many experiences with butterflies since Lyndsey passed that I know it is her way of giving us much-needed communication with her. It doesn't take away the pain of losing her, but it does give me hope that she lives on and we will be together again.

I get many notes of condolence on the anniversary of Lyndsey's passing from her friends and acquaintances. Many of them are now referring to that day as "Butterfly Day." The experiences with the butterflies have had a big impact all of them, not just our family.

I have had many more encounters with butterflies that I could share. I feel these stories need to be told so that they may be able to give someone else some comfort and hope as they endure the difficult journey of losing someone they love very much, especially if it is the worst loss of all, losing your child.

The butterfly was most likely a Short-Tailed Swallowtail, which is very similar to the Black Swallowtail. Black Swallowtails are found in Nova Scotia and New Brunswick but have never been recorded in Newfoundland. Below is a photo of a Tiger Swallowtail.

"I'm Here, and I'm Happy"

DESMA CHURCHILL

Portugal Cove, Newfoundland

I truly believe that butterflies are messengers from above. I have had a few interesting experiences with these graceful and elegant creatures. We lost our only child, Matthew, on March 28, 2005. On that day our world around us collapsed, and everything as we knew it came to an abrupt halt. As days turned into weeks, I prayed every day and night for some type of sign from Heaven above to let me know that Matthew was okay. "I'm here, and I'm happy" was what I needed to hear. I wished for pencils to move, or curtains to blow, or for a feather to drop at my feet. I prayed for my sign.

On July 14, 2005, what would have been Matthew's sixteenth birthday, I laid flowers and placed balloons at his resting place, and I again pleaded for a sign, a message from Matthew. "Please, Matthew," I said aloud, "send me just a little something—I'd like to see a butterfly." Within seconds of these words being said, the most beautiful butterfly I had ever seen landed upon Matthew's monument. I stood there and cried and thanked him for letting me know that he was okay, for sending his message of love. The butterfly didn't move until I left. As I headed back to my vehicle, the beautiful butterfly was following me. I smiled to myself. The graceful flutter of the butterfly had soothed my mind and spirit for a while.

Since this experience, a feeling of awe and peacefulness happens within me whenever I see a butterfly. People may think that I am a little crazy when I talk to the creatures and sometimes even follow them. We have a garden named after Matthew on our property that contains a butterfly bush gifted to us by friends, and now every summer we are visited by many Butterfly Messengers that bring us peace.

MATTHEW CHURCHILL

Butterfly Kisses

JO-ANNE DOOLING-DRAKE

Torbay, Newfoundland

Early in the spring of 2003 was a very extraordinary time for me. I had a wonderful sister, Vera, who passed from lung cancer. Over her last few months we had gotten very close. We exchanged stories of our childhood, hugged often, laughed as much as we could and exchanged our special "butterfly kisses." After her passing, I stayed close to my childhood friend Fern for comfort. We talked a lot about our losses as well as our gains over many cups of tea.

One sunny July evening, while sitting on my friend's front doorstep sipping our sugary tea, we reminisced some more. This time, the conversation was a little more lighthearted. We spoke of reincarnation and other signs from above. We took care in being respectful, and tried not to snicker too much.

Our eyes wandered around the neighbourhood. As we chatted, I spotted a huge black crow pitched on an overhead telephone wire. When we heard it call, Fern looked at me and said, "Sounds like your mother!" I said laughingly, "No, she would come back as a little barking dog." I laughed again.

During this lively conversation, a huge Red Admiral Butterfly came fluttering by. It soared and landed, then swooped all around us. The garden was rich in colourful flowers. We looked at each other in amazement. We had just been talking about my sister and her love of butterflies and our special "butterfly kisses." The beautiful butterfly came in around me, then landed so delicately on my foot. We froze in our conversation as the butterfly rested on my foot for a few seconds before flying off to explore again. Fern's face became more serious as she said in a daring voice, "If you are the spirit of Vera, land on her other foot."

We paused, holding our breath for just a second. The butterfly came swooping down again. It did not land on my foot, but settled itself down in front of my right one. We squealed with glee! In the midst of our excitement, a young girl from across the street came over looking for Fern's daughter, Jacky. Pulling her along on a long leash was a very tiny, fuzzy dog, that barked loudly and quite often. We couldn't even hear our own voices above the barking. The noise soon calmed down as Jacky and the little girl returned across the street, leaving just the two of us again. Before we could speak, the butterfly drifted away on another journey. We sat for another hour, chatting and sipping tea. I soon found myself at home again, deep within my thoughts of the day's events and how remarkable the butterfly's appearance was.

That Sunday morning when I awoke, the first thing I saw was my sister's picture on the wall. I decided to go to the local psychic fair to see what new and comforting information could unfold for me. I had had sessions with other readers in the past and always found them comforting. I had a great reading from a woman named Juliette. She assured me that my feelings about signs in nature, and how people, once passed, find ways to still be connected to their loved ones, were certainly very real. When I went home that day, I realized that it was July 20, and my sister's birthday was the nineteenth, the very day I had spent with my friend when the beautiful butterfly had landed on my foot. I also realized the connection with the little dog and how I had made reference to my mother coming back as a little barking dog. I called Fern and once again we had a great laugh about how strange and mysterious life can be.

"I Am Not Afraid"

HONNA AND DAVID HODDER
Paradise, Newfoundland

Our son, Matthew, was three years old when he was diagnosed with stage 4 neuroblastoma, a form of childhood cancer. For more than four years, he battled his disease with all the determination and bravery that a little one can manage. There was a brief period of remission which allowed him to have the experience of near normalcy. He attended kindergarten for a few months and even played T-ball for a little while. We allowed ourselves to think that we had won the war, though he certainly had returned with many scars from the front lines of the battlefield. When he relapsed we aggressively searched for all available options which offered some possibility of cure, while maintaining his quality of life. Matthew received various forms of treatment for his cancer both in Canada and the United States. Nothing worked, and his disease continued to progress. We were confronted with the reality that the most loving thing to do for our little man was to do all that was in our power to ease his suffering. Our hope transitioned painfully from a hope for a cure to a hope for a peaceful death.

The end came on September 3, 1997. Matthew had been receiving supportive palliative care from the Janeway Children's Hospital. I had carried him to the medical daycare unit the previous day for yet

another platelet transfusion. During the procedure, he experienced a seizure that terrified us both. I tried to comfort him as best I could, but he was so scared. He said, "Mommy, I can't see you." He had lost his vision completely. A moment later he had a second seizure. This one caused him to slip into a coma, from which he never recovered. His doctor moved us to a private room and his father and grandparents quickly came to be at his side. Matthew never again opened his eyes. For the next several hours we held him as his breathing became less and less.

What happened next can only be described as a miracle. Very slowly he said, "I am not afraid." A few minutes later, he was gone. Everybody in attendance witnessed this moment, including his nurse and pediatric oncologist.

The coming days were filled with grief and an over-whelming need to provide Matthew with a proper, dignified burial. It was at the funeral home that the butterflies came to me. It started when a relative arrived wearing a butterfly brooch. Actually, it wasn't that attractive, but I remember commenting on it. A few minutes later, someone handed me a card that included a small poem with a tiny butterfly pin inside. I still carry these things in my purse. As I was opening the card, a florist arrived with an arrangement in a ceramic butterfly bowl. It was at this point that I became overwhelmed with grief. In an effort to calm me, my husband took me to our car, which was in the parking lot. We sat there for a moment, lost in our pain. Then we heard a noise coming from the back seat. When we turned to look, there was a beautiful butterfly fluttering against the window. It was large and black with little spots of gold. I recall so vividly how shocked we were to see something so perfect present itself to us at our lowest possible point in life.

We took the appearance of the butterfly as a sign. It was a tiny offering of comfort that was held out to us to see us through the difficult time. We opened the window, but it didn't fly away. David climbed into the back seat and gathered it gently in his hands. I watched as he carried it to a nearby tree and set it on a branch. There it stayed for a few more moments before flying away.

To this day, we remember this peaceful experience. Though we would never need a reminder to keep our child alive in our hearts, we often whisper, "Hello, Matthew," whenever a butterfly flits by. In our minds, he is sending them to us to make us smile.

This is our story, as emotional as it has been to write. We would be honoured to have it shared with others who may also find peace in the midst of their grief.

A Small Glimmer of Hope

LIL CRITCH

When my nephew, Jack, got married a few years ago, he and his fiancée chose butterflies as their decorating theme. Eight months later, in April, Jack died under tragic circumstances. Of course, his wife was extremely distraught.

His funeral took place in a small community on the east coast. One can imagine how cold it was with the wind blowing off the Atlantic. When the funeral director opened the door of the hearse to remove the coffin, out flew a butterfly into his wife's face! She took this as a sign that Jack loved her and was with her, and it was a small glimmer of hope in an otherwise unbearable situation.

I See A Butterfly and Think of Her

CONNIE HAYWARD

St. John's, Newfoundland

Five years ago, on October 30, my dear friend passed away. She was more like a mother to me than just a friend. I had spent several months taking her for treatments and being the best support I could, but, sadly, her time came and she was gone.

A day or two after her passing, a beautiful butterfly was around our house most of the day. It was very unusual to see a butterfly in Newfoundland in November. I had never seen a butterfly at that time of year before and I haven't seen one so late in the season since. I mentioned the butterfly to her minister, and he used the story of the appearance of the butterfly in her eulogy.

I know in my heart that if there were any way for her to let me know that she was okay, she would do it, and now, I often see a butterfly in some form or another and think of her.

Aunt's Blessing

RHONDA GILBERT

My fiancé's aunt died one year before we were married. She loved butterflies and had them everywhere in her house. I had never met her, but members of her family told me that she would have liked me. For a full month before our wedding, I had a butterfly land on me every day while I was outside.

On my wedding day the same type of butterfly that I had been seeing landed on me and stayed there as I walked down the aisle. I have been married now for six years and, although I haven't had a butterfly land on me since, I believe it was my husband's aunt who was with me before the wedding and when I walked down the aisle. I believe she was giving us her blessing.

Dancing on the Rays of the Sun

LEIGH FORD

Kamloops, British Columbia

It was the summer of 2004. It had been such a rainy
one that I hardly remember seeing the sun. But there
wasn't much I could remember at that time, as there
was something heavier weighing on my mind, something that overpowered everything. My father was
dying of cancer. I was visiting my parents' home on
and off that summer, staying as long as I could, and
helping out in any way possible. The summer was long
and short, sad and happy, obtrusive and peaceful all at
the same time.

The doctors had been vague describing my father's
illness. It was a rare form of stomach cancer and we
were never really sure what stage he was in. I was opti-
mistic about it all. My father had always been so
healthy that I never believed he could ever die. Even
though I was an adult and had seen people pass away,
nothing about that summer convinced me that it
would happen then.

As his condition grew worse, I always assumed he
would get better, as he had always done. When he went
in to the hospital for the fourth time I knew he would
be out again, and I selfishly enjoyed the company who
had come from far off to visit. My father was born and
raised in Fogo, Newfoundland, and his sister and her

husband had come out to visit. It had been so many years since I had seen them that I wanted to spend every moment catching up.

On the second day of my father's hospital stay, my mother stayed with him while we all took the long ride home to the old ranch to rest. I was tired of sitting, of driving, of almost everything, and I expected my father home soon and knew the routine of staying up late with him would begin again. I leaned on the counter and tried to clear my head. I listened to the soft words of the people in conversation. I looked out through the French doors, past the covered deck, and out on to the lawn where the little apple tree stood, green from the rain. The grass was as green as it had ever been and the big poplars in the distance were lush in their foliage.

For the first time that day I noticed the sun, and then, something white and fluttering up and down. Between the apple tree and the deck, a white butterfly was dancing in the warm light of the sun. A white butterfly—had I ever seen a white butterfly before? I had grown up on the ranch, but my tired mind could hardly comprehend memories. I watched as the butterfly danced. Pure sunlight appeared to bounce off its wings. I wanted to smile. It moved up and down and in half-circles and mini-loops and I followed every movement it made. Then a heavy thump came from inside my chest and a surge of homesickness rose. Instantly I thought of Dad. *Did Dad just die, or is Dad feeling better? Did he just die and come back to me?* I swallowed.

Now, I couldn't look at the butterfly without thinking of my father, and I couldn't understand why. Then the butterfly flew off. I looked at the people in the room who were still talking. I looked at the phone beside me. Don't ring, I told it silently. But I couldn't shake the thought that there was something different now. The phone rang. It was Mom, telling me that Dad had just died. I hung up the phone and relayed the news to the room full of people. I turned to my aunt and said softly, "I just saw a white butterfly." With a serious face she said, "Maybe that was your father."

I don't know why I thought of Dad when I saw that white butterfly. My father, an ex-army officer and a hard-working and serious fellow, hardly prone to strange notions and certainly with no connection to butterflies, hardly seems to fit with what I saw or felt. I've never been drawn to butterflies or thought of them much over the years. I can't understand the connections, but everything in that moment was uncharacteristic and strangely mesmerizing and I still cannot explain exactly why. But I do know two things: that I have never felt that way looking at any animal before, let alone an insect, and that the shock that came from that call and the memories of my father being sick and dying of cancer have always slightly been buffered by images of that ballerina butterfly frolicking in a way my father never could have, healthy or not. To this day there is something inside me that believes for a moment my father was free from everything and he danced on the rays of the sun.

The Yellow Butterfly

WANDA GUSHUE

Pasadena, Newfoundland

In August of 1985, my maternal grandmother, who was approaching her ninety-third birthday, was hospitalized. Because of gangrene, the issue of lower leg amputation was discussed. Her three living children disagreed with this and refused to sign any consent papers. Hence, my grandmother, who always had a keen mind and super sharp memory, was heavily drugged. The drugs played havoc with her mind and she would chant her family history over and over, starting with, "My name is Jersha Knee," and refusing to let go of what she held dear, yet she could not connect the names that she was saying with the faces in front of her.

I spent a weekend visiting my grandmother that month, and every time that I went to the hospital I would don the same yellow dress with the hope that she would recognize me, or at least remember that I had been there after I returned home. Somehow, it worked! My mother, who stayed after I had left, told me that just a few days after my departure, a patient wearing a yellow housecoat crossed the hospital ward and my grandmother asked, "Is that Wanda?"

My darling grandmother passed away on September 16 of that year and was laid to rest on

September 19, just one day before her birthday. Her final resting place is Badger's Quay, Bonavista Bay.

On the day of her funeral, the most peculiar thing happened. When the undertaker did the token lowering of the coffin, I saw a big, beautiful, yellow butterfly that seemed to come from the centre of the grave and fly off to the southeast. Interestingly enough, when I later asked the family members who had been standing closer to the grave if they had seen the butterfly, not one of them had seen it. Yellow butterflies have been an item of interest to me ever since then.

I retired from teaching in June of 2009. On June 19 I was attending the retirement dinner hosted by the school board, and my good friend was going as my guest. As she sat on her patio waiting for me to get ready, a yellow butterfly, in her words, kept flying right toward her. She could not shoo the butterfly away, so finally she said, "Yes, Christopher, I know that you are here and I know that you are glad that I am filling in for you this evening." The butterfly then disappeared. My husband, Christopher, had passed away from Lou Gehrig's disease several years earlier.

Just a few days later, as we sat in on what would be my final meeting at school, my co-worker nodded toward the window and said, "Just look," and there was a beautiful yellow butterfly right at the window.

Then, several days ago, my older stepson and I were sitting on the patio reminiscing about Christopher and talking about his garden. Throughout the whole time, I kept seeing this yellow butterfly flitting about the garden. What is most interesting is that these are the only times that I have seen butterflies this summer. I feel so blessed!

It Always Brings Me Peace

ETHEL FRAMPTON

Paradise, Newfoundland

I have always been fascinated by butterflies for most of my life, and in the past few years, that fascination has increased. I have read that the adult butterfly symbolizes the freedom of the soul after death. In the western world, the symbol of the butterfly stands for freedom, naturalness, and purity. All of these things have become evident to me in the past few years since my husband died. After Mac's death, butterflies have become a symbol of peace and hope for me. He died in late fall, and the following summer I noticed more butterflies than usual around me, at times just hovering by my side.

The following fall, I was at the farmer's market buying vegetables for my family's Thanksgiving dinner. The farmer I was buying from suddenly looked at me and said, "Stand very still—don't move." Then he very quietly said, "Now turn your head very slowly and look on your right shoulder." There, sitting on my shoulder, was the most beautiful butterfly I had ever seen. It stayed there for a moment or two, then it just flew off and landed nearby on a huge pumpkin. We were both amazed, but I felt I knew just why that butterfly was there. It was there to tell me that Mac was at peace and happy, and that I was going to cook an amazing Thanksgiving dinner for our family. Family dinners and get-togethers were always important to him and something he had enjoyed immensely. I felt as though he was telling me to carry on with our traditions. It made my day and gave me a great feeling of peace and comfort.

Another time, while I was I approaching Mac's resting place on a visit to the cemetery, I noticed another beautiful butterfly sitting on his memorial stone. It stayed there for my entire visit and was still there as I walked away. This has happened on several different occasions.

Another incident occurred on my first solo visit to our summer cottage after his death. As I got out of my car and proceeded to walk up the steps to the door, a beautiful butterfly landed on the railing, as if to welcome me there. It stayed there, flitting around as I unloaded my things from my car and took them into the cottage, and lingered for quite a while afterward. Many times when I have been out gardening in my yard, and going back and forth from the backyard to the front of the house, a butterfly seemed to be just following me around. It always brings me peace. A few short years ago I got the opportunity to visit the Monarch Butterfly Sanctuary near Monterey, California. This is one of the places to which the Monarch Butterfly migrates for the winter.

I found it so peaceful just to sit there and see all those beautiful butterflies in the huge California trees. It is really amazing—another wonder of this world. As I sat there that day I visualized just seeing all those butterflies leave the trees to fly around. What a wonderful sight it was!

Six Years Old
When He Lost His Daddy

IRENE JACOBS

Badger's Quay, Newfoundland

On September 21, 2004, my husband and I lost our only son, Craig, in a tragic car accident near Badger. Craig was thirty-one years old and so full of life that he was an inspiration to all of our family, especially his son, Brandon, who was only six years old when he lost his daddy.

It is said that when we lose someone close to us, our sense of environment and our surroundings is heightened. We tend to notice the smaller things in life and appreciate them more. My husband and I have had numerous experiences where a butterfly or bird has brought us comfort, or a sense of peace when it was needed most. Sometimes, we would be sitting on our patio at our cottage talking about our memories of Craig, when a butterfly would fly by, just in front of us, linger for a moment, and then fly off into the sky. In one instance in particular, we were at the cabin when a butterfly appeared and stayed with us for a while. It was flying around us, and then flew a little farther away, but kept returning. At one point, the butterfly pitched on my arm. It was amazing to see it up so close; I could see every detail of its black and orange wings. Eventually, it took flight and disappeared.

These experiences with Butterfly Messengers have touched our hearts in a way we could never explain.

Another experience that has been very meaningful to us, and we will never forget: this Butterfly Messenger came to us on August 4, 2007. It was our niece Renee's wedding day. Renee and Craig had been very close. They spent much of their childhood together and remained close friends into their adult years. Renee was a bridesmaid at Craig's wedding, and it was her intention that Craig stand at hers as well. But tragically, Craig passed away before he could fulfill that role.

On Renee's wedding day, she had 100 live butterflies shipped in from Quebec to be released in memory of family members and friends who had passed on. The butterflies were distributed to some of the guests, and on the count of three, they were all released from their individual cardboard boxes. Ninety-nine butterflies took to the sky immediately. The one butterfly that I was releasing did not. Instead, it landed on my dress, sat there a moment, and then landed on Brandon's tie, then flew back and pitched on my arm. The rest of the butterflies were long gone, off into the sky, but this one butterfly continued to stay with us, eventually landing in Brandon's hands. Eventually, the guests were leaving and my husband told Brandon that it was time to let the butterfly go. Brandon lifted his hands to the sky, and the butterfly took flight and was gone. It was such an overwhelming experience for us all, and it was surreal that the butterfly had stayed with us for so long. Our Butterfly Messenger left my family and me with the belief that it was Craig, telling us he is still with us always.

"A Butterfly This Time of Year"

MARY AND HERMAN AVERY

St. John's, Newfoundland

My husband, Herman, and I live in St. John's. I have to start by saying that neither of us knew anything about Butterfly Messengers. A few weeks ago, my son had gone to Western Bay with his girlfriend, like he did every other weekend. On October 13, at 6:45 a.m., we received a call informing us that he had died. You can imagine our shock. We rushed to be with his girlfriend and her family, and then back home to make the necessary arrangements for the funeral. It has been an extremely hard time. He was just thirty-five years old, and we were told that he died of a massive heart attack.

Prior to his death, my son had given me a beautiful butterfly brooch that I said I would cherish always. On October 29, his girlfriend and her parents visited us at our house. It was a beautiful day but very cold. My kitchen has a patio door with a window. While everyone was chatting, a beautiful butterfly flew twice into the glass of the door and again into the window. It was only my husband and I and her father who noticed our visitor. I made the comment, "Imagine seeing a butterfly this time of year!" My son's girlfriend had been talking and did-n't know about the butterfly.

Several days later, my husband was speaking with my son's girlfriend. In the conversation, he mentioned seeing the butterfly that day. She said, "I can't believe you are telling me this—I have something to show you." She showed him a story in the newspaper about Butterfly Messengers, and Herman brought it home to show me. It was only then that I realized the butterfly at our window that day may not just have been an odd sight, but a message from above.

Ryan's Favourite Colour

KELLY STOYLES-HICKS

My son, Ryan, died of neuroblastoma cancer two years ago. You would have to know my son just to understand how special he was—he was truly a beautiful soul. Ryan was diagnosed at the tender age of three and fought hard until he lost his battle on August 25, 2007. Ryan's favourite colour was orange.

The day of his funeral, we requested that everyone wear something orange, and as the funeral car drove away after the Mass, we released hundreds of orange balloons into the sky. Later, as family members gathered at the house, my husband and I took a walk down to the river on our property, which was a very special place for Ryan. There, we encountered hundreds of orange butterflies just resting on the bushes. It was the most unbelievable sight; they were so peaceful. We told other family members and they proceeded to go look at this majestic sight. I think this was truly a special gift from Ryan.

Another event followed a month after his death, on my fortieth birthday; Ryan was big on birthdays, especially mine. He would go around for days whispering with his dad, give me a gold plastic medal, like the ones you give kids at birthday parties, and would always pick out something special for me. On this day, to occupy my time, I went out and did some gardening, something

36

unusual for me. But that day will always remain close to my heart as an orange butterfly appeared and followed my around the garden. It just fluttered around me! I walked from one side of the house to the other and this butterfly went with me. I felt that Ryan was with me, and it made the day easier to bear.

Several members of my family have experienced similar occurrences since Ryan died, an orange butterfly that always seemed to appear out of nowhere just when it is needed. Butterflies are now a big part of our lives, just as Ryan was and always will be.

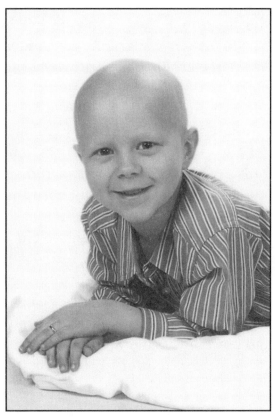

RYAN STOYLES-HICKS

"That's Kasey, Keeping An Eye On Us"

PATRICIA E. LACEY

Torbay, Newfoundland

On July 24, 2006, my niece, Janet Allen, and her daughter, Kasey, were killed in a tragic accident just outside of Deer Lake, Newfoundland. Whenever Janet and her husband took their family on holidays, they always tried to take the children to educational places, such as the Insectarium. They had visited there that very day.

Kasey, my grandniece, had always loved butterflies. On June 20 and 21 this past summer, my girlfriend and I hiked the Spout Trail, part of the East Coast Trails. When we were part of the way down Shoal Bay Road, a small butterfly with blue wings kept flying around me, zigzagging in and out of the woods but always staying in my sight. The butterfly stayed with us as we walked along the coastline until we set up camp that night. I said to my girlfriend, "That's Kasey, keeping an eye on us." I kept thinking about Kasey and her love of butterflies and my love for her and her mom. I knew her mother would soon surface to me as a butterfly, because they were together now.

The next morning while hiking again, we were going up a steep incline when a big yellow butterfly landed on a tree branch in front of me, and I knew then that it was Janet taking over for Kasey on the rough terrain. She stayed with us most of the day, but I guess she had to leave eventually to go check on Kasey. What beautiful butterflies they were!

To this day, whenever I see butterflies I always say a little prayer for Janet and Kasey.

The next story, from my hometown of Pasadena, is very touching but also has a bit of humour built in. The author asked me to drop by his home and record his story. I have to admit we had a good chuckle when we got to the end. While the story is not meant to be humorous, his way of preserving his sister's memory certainly is.

"Sis"

RENDELL DROVER
Pasadena, Newfoundland

My sister, Joyce, was seventy-one when she passed away from cancer on September 26, 1997. Anyone who knew Joyce was aware that she loved butterflies. She had known her cancer was terminal and she had made many of the preparations for her own funeral. She prepared an outline of the bulletin to be used, complete with a picture of a butterfly on the front, and she even changed one of the hymns so that there was a reference to a butterfly. The funeral service was held in Clarenville, so my family and I drove across the island from our home in Pasadena.

We attended the very touching church service and then everyone went to the cemetery. Just before the start of the graveside prayers, they lowered the casket halfway down and then proceeded with the burial service. All of a sudden, a beautiful butterfly appeared. It fluttered about throughout the crowd and swooped down around the casket. We thought it was a significant sign, given Joyce's love of butterflies.

The day after the funeral, we drove back to Pasadena and stopped at a restaurant in Badger for some lunch. Our daughter Jennifer was travelling with us, and when we all got out of our car we noticed a butterfly on the rail of the restaurant. I went over to the the butterfly and reached out my hand and the butterfly crawled up onto my arm. My daughter came over and we touched arms, and the butterfly climbed onto her and crawled all the way up her arm, and, after a short time, flew away. We felt that Joyce was keeping an eye on us while we made our journey home. We continued on to Pasadena and arrived sometime in the afternoon. My wife, Jean, decided to wash some clothes, and as she was hanging the last item on the line, a butterfly came and landed on this last item of clothing, which we thought was very unusual.

The next day I did a little painting on the outside of the house, and as I was sitting down having a little break, a butterfly came and started flying all around me. I was talking to the butterfly, and at that point I started calling it "Sis." I truly felt that the butterfly was my sister Joyce, coming to pay me a friendly visit. The butterfly continued to hang around throughout the fall.

Time went quickly, and before we knew it, it was Christmas. We burn wood to supplement our heating, and we have a woodshed outside and keep a woodbox in the rec room close to the stove. A butterfly must have gotten into the woodshed during the fall and came into the house when we brought in the wood.

Jean and I were downstairs one night, enjoying the heat from the wood stove. Jean went upstairs to get ready for bed. All of a sudden a butterfly came out of the woodbox and started flying all around the room. I called out to my wife, "Come on down and see who's here!" She finished what she was doing and came down, expecting that some friend had dropped by for a Christmas visit. In the meantime, the butterfly had crawled in behind a model boat I had in the rec room and disappeared. She said, "What are you talking about?" I said, "Just wait a minute and you'll see." The butterfly then flew out and she was shocked. We both stood there and the butterfly flew all around us.

I had a picture on the wall that represented the history of the Drover family. The butterfly flew up to the top of the picture and crawled in behind the frame. I thought, if this was Joyce visiting us, she certainly picked an appropriate symbol to let us know it was her. The picture was so tight to the wall that you could actually see it moving as the butterfly crawled down behind. It then crawled all the way to the bottom, and that's where it stayed for the night.

I was working at the Deer Lake Airport at the time, and in the morning I went down to the rec room before I left for work, to say, "Good morning, Sis," to the butterfly. The butterfly would flutter its wings when I spoke to it. In the evening, as soon as I got my boots off, down I would go and speak to "Sis" again.

This went on for three or four days, until I came home one day from work and my son Michael said, "She's gone, Dad." I said, "No, she can't be gone, there is no way for her to get out of the house." I went around and, after a while, I found her behind the picture again. I lifted the frame and out she came. She flew all around and then back into the woodbox, where she came from in the first place. I said, "You can't stay there, you might get hurt." I went to take her out, but she flew out herself. She fluttered around for a while, and then she landed on top of the television. There was a hat nearby that belonged to our son, so I took the hat and put it over her. I said, "There, that will keep you safe for the night," and we all went to bed. The hat turned out to be a big mistake! The heat from the television was too much for the butterfly, and the next day, when I went to say good morning to her, I found that she had died.

I felt so bad about losing the butterfly that I decided to take it to work with me, and that day I had a brilliant idea. We had a small laminating machine at work, and I decided to laminate the butterfly, so that I could keep her forever. That was thirteen years ago, and I have carried her around with me in my wallet ever since. I still call her "Sis!"

Since then, the visits from butterflies have continued. When I work in my shed, the butterflies come and actually fly right into the shed with me. I feel my sister is with me all the time, and I have no doubt that it is really her. Having the butterfly in my wallet every day helps me to feel that much closer to her.

"Hello Little Butterfly. Are You Lost?"

SHIRLEY FROST

Lower East Pubnico, Nova Scotia

It was September 1993, about a month after our beloved daughter Susan's sudden and tragic death. My husband and I were walking along the sand dunes at the beach near our home in Nova Scotia with her three little children, Maria, four, Megan, three, and Joshua, one. The wind was soft and warm, the kind of day when the world seems quiet and gentle. The kind of day when you wonder how can it be that the world is still revolving, yet your heart is breaking and your soul is troubled.

A little white butterfly began to flit around us, first before us, and then behind us, then seemed to want to fly along with us. Maria began to speak to the butterfly in a voice too old, wise and wistful to come from the mouth of a child. "Hello, little butterfly. Are you lost? I know why you are following us, and I know what you are thinking. You are wondering where your mommy is, aren't you?" Transposed grief, I knew, in the only way a little child can speak. Some grief is too painful to be spoken of in the first person; but a child finds a way.

As we watched, Maria's hands formed a cup, inviting the butterfly to come to her. The butterfly flitted about, and the children were delighted. "Jesus knows Mommy, you know. She went to Heaven to live with Him," Megan suddenly stated reassuringly, in a matter-of-fact voice. "Yes," I replied. Maria sadly looked away and nodded in agreement. "Mommy!" Josh cried out suddenly. At the age of one, the sound of her name seemed to stir a warm and wonderful memory of something within him that he was not quite sure of. He didn't say anything else, but tears filled his eyes to the brim of his long, dark lashes and rolled soundlessly down his cheeks.

Again I told them how very much their mommy loved them, and how she still does. I tell them their daddy loves them, and that Papa and I love them and everyone else in the family will love them forever and ever. I tell them that they will never be alone, ever, and that Jesus loves them, and that they are so, so precious to us.

Megan, being the family philosopher, decided to make a wish, "a wish that nothing bad ever happens again, so now it won't," in a voice so convincing that even I believed her. The little butterfly hovered, then spun away. "Goodbye, little butterfly," we laughed as it swirled into the sky. Maria's blue eyes sparkled, and she looked at her little sister and brother protectively, expectantly, pleased with herself. "We are going to be okay, we are," my husband and I told them.

We ran through the dunes to the water's edge, where even the waves were subdued. We waded along the shoreline and suddenly felt joyful again. Josh threw pebbles and we ducked to avoid being hit; he laughed hilariously as we exaggerated running away from him. White waves washed over tiny feet, and everyone was smiling.

45

That little butterfly had done her work. She had opened the lines of communication to heal tender broken hearts and brought us joy in that time of sorrow.

I have never seen a white butterfly since without being reminded of that wonderful day on the beach when a lone butterfly brought a grieving child a tangible gift in a spirit of love—truly a gift from mother to child, from child to child, and then on to me.

Dad's Swing Set

JENNY PENNEY

Salmon Cove, Newfoundland

My father, Jim Butt, of Carbonear, Newfoundland, passed away on October 7, 2006, and was buried on Thanksgiving Day, October 9. We were very close while I was growing up, and people always said we were a lot alike. We had a lot of the same interests, especially with reading books and talking about them together. We were always carrying on and joking around. A lot of the time we never even had to say much to each other. He was like a best friend besides being my father, because I could talk to him and asked his advice on decisions I had to make.

On October 4, 2007, I was having a bad day because I was missing Dad a lot, and it was getting close to being a year since he had passed away. That morning, I was looking out my bedroom window when a butterfly came and landed right on the window. It stayed there for the longest time. I got my camera and took a picture so I could have it to keep and look at every now and then. I felt like it had come to cheer me up.

A few months before Dad had passed away, I bought him a swing set to put outside for him and Mom to sit on and enjoy. Exactly a year after Dad died, on October 7, Thanksgiving Day, my brothers, sister, and I went to Mom's house for dinner. I went outside to go and sit in his swing, and as I was walking toward it I saw a butterfly resting on the front of the seat. I got really excited because I was thinking that it was a way of cheering me up and letting me know that Dad was still with us on this special day. I always have my camera on me; I happily took another picture to keep with all of his things.

Emma's Orange Butterfly

EMMA GRIFFITHS

Placentia, Newfoundland

My life has been blessed with three marvellous Butterfly Messengers. After dealing with the death of my sister, who passed away with breast and lung cancer and to whom I was extremely close, I was myself diagnosed with the same disease. Daily, I prayed for an orange butterfly to find out if she was hearing from me, but told no one about my wish.

Two weeks passed by, and one day I received a card from my friend in Toronto, a friend I hadn't seen for a long time. In the card was a beautiful cardboard butterfly. Shortly after receiving this card, I was visiting a friend. When I was leaving, he said he had something for me. It was a picture he had taken in his garden of a beautiful butterfly on his lilac tree. The picture now hangs on my wall, where I can admire it every day.

A few times last summer, I sat on my patio, and each time I did, an orange butterfly would perch on the chair next to me. It would stay there until I left, and I felt comforted by it and would talk to it as if I was talking to my dear sister.

"I Would Love to Be A Butterfly"

BETTY NORMORE

L'Anse-au-Loup, Labrador

I have so many stories about butterflies that I think I could write a book! To begin, we lost our fourteen-year-old daughter, Paula, on January 19, 2001. Shortly after her death, I found pages and pages of material that she had written. She left behind so many beautiful words and stories. She had actually written her autobiography, and it was amazing. One quote was, "I'd like to be a butterfly because they are beautiful and have many colours like the rainbow. They can also fly to the sky, and I would love to be able to fly and have beautiful colour . . . therefore, I would love to be a butterfly!"

I have a butterfly incorporated into her monument, and it is beautiful. She had a mirror in her school locker shaped like a butterfly, she had an appliqué on her jeans shaped like a butterfly, and the list goes on and on!

We decided to hold benefit fundraisers after her accident, around her birthday, which was September 10, and of course almost everything we sold had something to do with butterflies—quilts, stickers, magnets, mugs, and so on. We donated the funds to the Children's Wish Foundation and another charity of our choice. We did this for five years in a row. Then my uncle, who had always emceed these events, developed cancer and passed away, so that was the end of our fundraisers.

During the first fundraising event that we held, I was having a very difficult time, and I went outside and asked Paula for a sign. There was a butterfly, and it flew around and around me and landed on a little bridge in our backyard. I went up to it, and as I knelt there, I actually stroked the butterfly and talked to it. I know it was Paula!

PAULA NORMORE

Another incident happened when Paula's father, Dennis, and I were having a rough time. We decided to get away for a few days and go to the Gros Morne National Park area. One of the things we did was hike the Gros Morne Mountain. As we neared the summit, the climbing became very difficult on the loose rock. I cried out to Paula and asked her if this was the right thing to be doing, and just ahead of us appeared two butterflies frolicking around and around. I always have my camera, and I got photos of both of them.

Another time, I went outside and a butterfly landed on my shirt and I could not get it off. I am so sure that these butterflies were our angels letting us know that they are okay. In the past few days during my walks, I saw butterflies everywhere.

We recently lost another teenager close to us, and his mother told me that, while on a walk, a butterfly followed her the whole way. We are not losing our minds—we are just in tune with our angels! Many people here on the south coast of Labrador have told me that they think about Paula when they see a butterfly.

My brothers were ice fishing the same winter that she had her accident, and a butterfly flew around and around their snowmobile—this is unheard of right in the middle of the winter!

On what would have been Paula's twenty-third birthday, it was a constant battle of the minds to decide whether or not to even go in to work that day, but I decided to put on my mask and go for it. It was very hard when I would think about her and have to put my mind elsewhere, but I did it. I am an LPN and I work at a clinic/long-term care facility. As I was feeding one of the residents, I happened to glance out the window, and there were butterflies flying around everywhere! I smiled to myself and went on with my work. As I sat to eat in the dining room at work, I could see a butterfly at the window several times, but again I just chuckled to myself.

At the end of my shift, as I sat in our nursing office to give my daily report, a butterfly came out of nowhere and landed on the worksheet that I had in my hand. Myself and all five of my co-workers stared at it in wonder. One of the girls said, "Oh my God, Betty, a butterfly today!" I just very calmly walked outside with it and watched as it flew off! I said, "You guys can believe what you like, but I know that this was Paula showing me that it was all right to go to work today!"

Yellow Butterfly Saves Lives

ROXANN DALTON

Ridgefield, Connecticut

My fourteen-year-old niece, Paula Normore, passed away on January 19, 2001. After her passing, her mother found some letters and papers she had written for school. In one letter, she had written that she would love to be a butterfly. After she died it seemed that butterflies were turning up everywhere, and this soon became a symbol for the darling little girl that we had lost.

One afternoon I was driving home on a busy interstate highway in North Carolina. My thoughts were filled with all the things I needed to accomplish, what I didn't get done today, and what needed to be done at home. I was driving quite fast and wasn't paying attention to what I was doing, when all of a sudden a huge yellow butterfly passed directly in front of my car. There was no way I could have missed seeing it. I smiled and thought of Paula. I realized that I had been driving very fast and then made a point of slowing down my car. At the moment when I saw the butterfly, I was coming off the interstate and approaching a green light at an intersection. Just as I was about to cross the intersection, a large truck ran straight through the red light going the other way. If I had not slowed down after seeing the butterfly, I would have been right in the path of the truck that ran the red light. But because I had seen the butterfly and slowed down, that couple of extra seconds saved my life and the lives of my two little boys sitting in the back seat. I have no doubt that Paula was watching over me that day and, in her own way, she saved our lives.

I still see butterflies every day. Sometimes they fly in front of me, sometimes just around us, but I know in my heart of hearts that it's my own angel, Paula, letting me know she's still around.

The Intervention

JOHN REID

Kanata, Ontario

As a teenager, my son David had a summer job mowing lawns in the neighbourhood. One afternoon, he was cutting the narrow strip of grass between two residential homes, when a butterfly with unimaginable colours and markings landed on the handle of the lawnmower as he was walking. He paused briefly to admire this little beauty when a bundle of shingles slid off the roof of one of the homes and slammed to the ground right in front of the lawnmower. The shingles would have surely landed on David had the butterfly not appeared—seriously injuring him, or worse.

David has since become an Emergency First Responder with a penchant of being at the right place at the right time. To his credit, he has saved the lives of many people, including a seven-day-old infant—all, you might say, made possible due to the intervention of an unusual butterfly one summer afternoon.

I Idolize the Butterfly

SHIRLEY MAXINE GAUDET
Halifax, Nova Scotia

The ringing of the phone roused me from a deep sleep. I had gone to bed early and I certainly wasn't expecting a phone call. I reached over and picked up the phone and managed a sleepy hello. My daughter Susan was on the line. She said, "Mom, are you in bed? Is the door locked? We're over at the pay phone and we'll be there in a few minutes." I jumped out of bed and grabbed my housecoat, hurriedly put it on and ran down the stairs. Just as I was unlocking the door, I saw my two daughters and their husbands. One of them was holding my two-month-old granddaughter. I said a prayer of thanksgiving when I saw her, for my biggest fear was that something had happened to her.

We all came into the kitchen and I asked, "What is going on? Why are you here at this hour on a week night?" Susan said, "Mom sit down, please, we have some bad news . . . Grammy is dead." "No, that can't be," I cried loudly, "she was here only three weeks ago and she was fine!"

Angela said, "Mom, Aunt Margo called a couple of hours ago. She didn't want to tell you over the phone, so she asked us to come here and tell you in person, and so we could be with you at this terrible time."

My mother had been complaining of a sore arm for

some days, but when my sister suggested she go to the doctor, she said it was only her arthritis and it would go away on its own as it always did. Unfortunately, that didn't happen this time. She called Linda, the daughter who lived closest to them, and asked her to take her up to the clinic.

Upon arrival at the local medical clinic, she was examined and it was determined that she should go to the hospital in St. John's by ambulance. My sister Linda accompanied her, and sometime during the trip, the apparatus that was connected to her went "berserk," as my sister described it. She cried out to the nurse that something was wrong, but she was told that everything was okay, and that they would soon be at the hospital. Shortly afterward, they did arrive at the hospital and were quickly escorted to an emergency room. The verdict was already in. Mom had died. In the meantime our sister Margo, who was a nurse, had been notified of what was happening. She was rushed to the hospital to be with Linda. Everyone was overcome with grief, but they handled the situation to the best of their ability. Our father was the biggest concern, of course. He had to be told, and there was no getting around that fact.

Since I wasn't there, I can't be entirely sure of what exactly took place. But pieced together, it was a very sad story.

My daughter Susan and I left Halifax Airport early in the morning. We were met by my sisters at the St. John's Airport, and they took us home to South Dildo. The family was gathered around. Even my brother, who was living in Texas, was there with his new wife.

My youngest son, Michael, arrived from his home in Montreal later in the day. He was a tremendous help to us all. He kept the younger children entertained with his stories and drawings of them, and they loved that.

Everyone seemed to be walking around in a daze. Someone took us up to Norman's Cove, which was my mothers birthplace, as well as my own. My mother was at the church she had attended as a child, spending her last earthly rest. When I walked up to the open casket, I was amazed at the look on my mother's face. She seemed to me to be wearing sort of a half-smile and looking entirely at peace. I, too, for a moment felt a sense of peace—a feeling that she was in a better place.

The funeral was held the next day, on my fifty-second birthday. My mother would have been seventy-two on her next birthday, which was October 19. She wasn't quite twenty years old when I was born, and I was her second child. She went on to have eight more children, all except one still living at that time, September 1985.

After the funeral, we went to my sister's home in Hopeall, a small community just down the shore from the family home in South Dildo. When I awoke the next morning, I finally realized that my beloved mother was gone, and I would never see her again. I recalled the happy times we'd had together that summer, while she and her sister Margo and her son Andre visited me at my home in Nova Scotia, where I worked as a schoolteacher. Because I had the summer off, we had all the time we wanted to wander around and do all the things she loved to do. Shopping, visiting her grandchildren, eating out, and attending a show at the university where I graduated from—these were some of the things that we did. My youngest daughter, Cheryl, was performing at the university, which made it even more exciting for my mother.

I sensed that I was the only one up, so I decided to go down to the beach for a walk to try to get myself under control. When I arrived at the beach, the wind was blowing a gale, the seagulls barely holding their own as they floundered about in the turbulence. I ran along the beach, screaming my mother's name and pleading with her to come back. If anyone had heard my cries, they probably would have thought I was crazy—and I probably was, a little. I stopped to get my breath, and saw a beautiful butterfly that had landed upon a wild rose bush. I was suddenly entranced, and reached out to touch it. Before I could reach it, it flew away. I followed it, but time and time again when I came within reach, it would take flight again. I couldn't understand how such a tiny creature could control its movements under such windy conditions. Suddenly, a feeling of peace came over me, and I knew that my mother was safe and in a better place, where she would have no more pain or sorrow—only happiness and love while she waited for the rest of us to join her and all the other members of our family who had gone on before her.

When I turned to leave my chase for the butterfly, I was stunned to see my son coming toward me. He had come down to the beach after discovering my absence at the house. He knew my habits well enough to know that I would be at the beach under the circumstances. We rushed to each other and embraced. He told me that he was concerned about me and decided to come looking for me. He had watched my unsuccessful quest for the butterfly, and had been amused by it. When we returned to the house, I tried to explain the significance of the butterfly to him. He, too, was in awe of it. Other members of the family were not so easily convinced that a simple butterfly could possibly be such a significant sign. Over the years, though, they came to believe as I did.

I believe the butterfly symbolized my mother's spirit. I also believe that, since I was her eldest daughter, she chose to have the messenger sent to me, knowing that I would convey the message to the rest of the family. At first they were skeptical. Now, after all these years, we all agree that the butterfly was our mother's way of letting us know that she was safe and that she loved us all.

To this very day, I idolize the butterfly in all its forms. I never send a greeting card to any of my children, grandchildren, or sisters unless it features a beautiful butterfly, and they always do the same for me.

This event happened twenty-three years ago, but it is as fresh in my memory today as if it had happened yesterday.

"Stay There Until I Get Back"

LIZ PINSENT

St. John's, Newfoundland

My dad passed away on September 25, 2007. A short time later, my mom experienced something that she will never forget. My sister had been staying at Mom's house to help her through a hard grieving period. They were in bed one night chatting about what to do with their car. Mom didn't think she would ever drive again and was thinking about selling it. My sister told her that maybe she should wait and see how she felt about it in a few months.

Following the conversation, Mom went to use the washroom. She stopped on the way to look out the window and could not believe what she saw. My sister's car was covered with frost and snow, but mom's car had no snow on it at all. However, on the roof of the car, there was frost in the shape of a butterfly that covered the entire roof like crystals of ice. My mom was in shock, as she had heard stories about butterflies in the past and now thought to herself, "Wow, they have to be true!"

She called my sister and told her, but she didn't believe what Mom was saying. She got up and went to the window. She was amazed at the sight, and as tears rolled down her face she turned to my mother and said, "Mom, I would have not believed you if I didn't see it for myself." They both thought that it was Dad telling her not to sell the car. Mom decided to keep it after all, and still drives it daily.

After my father passed away, my sister would take her son and our mom to try to get out of the house every day and ease the grief they were all feeling. One day, as they were on their way out, Mom noticed a butterfly on the flowers by the side of the front door, where she and Dad would sit for hours on a nice day. She started talking to the butterfly. She had heard that the butterfly is a sign that a loved one who has died is close by and free from pain. Mom said, "Harry, if that's you, flap your wings," and the butterfly fluttered its wings on the flower but did not fly away. Mom was amazed. My sister was getting impatient and said, "Come on, Mom, let's go. If that's Dad, he'll be there when we get back." Mom thought for a moment and said, "Harry, if that's you, stay there until I get back, please."

They were gone for a few hours. When they returned from their drive, the butterfly was still there, sitting on the same flower. Mom tried to reach and touch it, but it flew away. A lot of times when the weather is nice, the butterfly comes back to that flower. We all say it's Dad's way of telling us that he is free from pain, and still close by.

"Look, There's Grandma"

FIONA FRAWLEY

Goose Bay, Labrador

My mother passed away from cancer in March 2007. During the two years she battled cancer, she would tell my son, Daniel, now fourteen, that she would always be a part of his life, just in a different form. She had always loved butterflies, and we weren't surprised when she told us that she would come back as a butterfly. In her final letter to my son, she told him to think of her whenever he saw a butterfly.

The first Mother's Day without her was extremely difficult. Imagine our surprise that day when my son looked out on the patio and exclaimed, "Look, there's Grandma!" We looked out and, sure enough, there was a butterfly flying around our patio! Of course, some would dismiss it as coincidental, but we do live in Goose Bay, and it is pretty unusual to have butterflies around at that time of the year!

This year on Mother's Day we decided to go out and spend the day geocaching. Just as we stepped out of the vehicle, my son remarked, "I guess Grandma decided to visit us today!" Sure enough, there was a butterfly flying around him! I don't think both experiences can be dismissed as coincidental! I'm not too sure whether there is an afterlife in a religious sense; however, I firmly believe that there is another level of being after death. I find it very comforting when I see a butterfly, because one usually seems to show up when we are low in spirit, and I don't doubt for a moment that it's my mother's way of saying, "Oh for goodness' sake, what are you moping about, I'm still around when you need me!" Other family members and friends have also reported seeing butterflies at the oddest of times and in the oddest of places since her passing.

"I'll Visit You As A Butterfly"

EMMIE PENNEY

Pasadena, Newfoundland

Several years before my mother passed away in 2004, at the age of ninety, I would pester her about how I hoped she would give me a sign after she had gone. She knew I believed in the ability of people to make contact once they passed over. I never did determine if she believed in this as well. Finally, one day during another of our conversations, she said, "All right, Emmie, all right, I'll visit you as a butterfly." At the time, I felt she had said it more to keep me quiet than anything else. When Mom passed after several months of illness, I was away at a gift show in Toronto and felt dreadful that I wasn't with her when she died. The day of her funeral in August was a beautiful sunny day. When we returned from the church, four or five family members were standing on my back patio. Along came a beautiful butterfly and perched right on the door entrance to the house. It stayed there for an unusually long time before flying away. I know it was a sign from Mom, letting us know that she was happy in another place.

More recently, this past summer, as my sister, Daphne, and I were climbing Gros Morne Mountain, we discovered a butterfly following us for about ten minutes as we made the climb up the slope. My sister and I were excited to see the butterfly so high up the mountain and joked that it was Mom looking out for us. After following us for more than ten minutes, it then pitched on my sister several times, on her leg, her foot, and her shoulder, and managed to pitch on me once as well. In our hearts, we feel certain it was Mom's way of reaching out to us once again.

Fidelis House

GERTRUDE MORSE
Centreville, Nova Scotia

My girlfriend, Shirley, died on November 7, 1988, after a long battle with leukemia, which she had battled for nearly a decade. She was fifty years old at the time. Before her death, she had acquired a book on butterflies and had asked her friends to pick the one they would identify with. She had always said that she would like to come back as a butterfly, since they are so beautiful and free. She felt trapped by her illness, as indeed she was. My chosen butterfly was, and is still, the Monarch. My friend's dream had been to establish a house for people who were either receiving treatment, as she had been, or for families of those ill in the hospital, so that they could stay in close proximity to the hospital and be near their loved ones.

The house, that she had wanted to call Fidelis House (Fidelis was named for her mother), was initially established by the Lion's Club of Kentville, NS. It took four years to raise sufficient funds to get it up and running, initially within the Miller Hospital. It remained there for ten years until the place was torn down. Since that time we have built a new house with twelve rooms, and it is operated entirely by volunteers.

On the day of the grand opening of the new house, as the speeches were being given, a very large Monarch

Butterfly appeared out of nowhere and zoomed over-head, circled once, and then disappeared.

Recently, Shirley's mother was dying while I was in Florida, and as I was coming out of a restaurant, two Monarch Butterflies flew over, circled and disappeared. I was stunned and suddenly realized that it was Shirley, coming to meet her mother. The date was Friday, January 30, and Fidelis died the next day.

Butterflies Have Been My Guide

HOLLY SMITH

St. John's, Newfoundland

Butterflies—beautiful, fragile, mystical . . . and oh so powerful. I've always received a certain comfort from their presence, even as a small girl gathering them gently, keeping them if only for a few quiet moments in a well-ventilated container, then setting them free to float the skies and send their special messages.

I remember in my early adulthood receiving a gift of a beautiful yellow and black butterfly, crafted to sit steadfastly on my bedroom wall at home, where it provided a distraction and almost an inspiration through my early adult life. I kept that special friend dusted until its wings faded and frayed. It was finally put to rest when I spread my wings and moved away from home.

A few short years later, on my wedding day, my husband (though we had agreed not to exchange gifts) gave me a beautiful gold butterfly pendant encrusted with tiny diamonds. I just looked in awe, as he was totally unaware of my special affection for these wonderful winged friends. I wear it proudly to this day after twenty-seven years.

My in-laws lived in a house by the sea in Cupids, Newfoundland, where we spent plenty of leisure time. Our two children played happily in the long grass chasing each other and, of course, the beautiful butterflies appeared from time to time, always using the nets I had purchased at a local store. The nets came with well-ventilated containers and a magnifying glass for collecting. They, too, treated the butterflies with kindness and always remembered to release them back into their carefree world, without a trace of disrespect. My children grew to be fine adults of whom we are very proud.

My mother-in-law and father-in-law were enjoying their golden years in Cupids when Gramma became stricken with Alzheimer's disease. It often became necessary to distract and guide her thought patterns to avoid behaviour escalation or even catastrophe. One afternoon, we put on our warm jackets, I linked my arm into hers, and we went outside to visit her garden, which was her pride and joy. It was very early in the spring, the tulips had just started peeping out of the soil. The chill from the ocean kept us huddled together to keep warm. I kept thinking, *How are we going to get through this?* Gramma had been going downhill for the past few weeks, and we all feared for Grampy's health as well. We knew all too well what lay ahead. It seemed to just appear out of nowhere—a single butterfly gently gliding toward us, not at all timid. It approached us and lingered long enough to catch Gramma's short-term attention, and she paused to admire its colour and beauty. It floated in front of and around us for several minutes, and Gramma was captured by its beautiful yellow and black display. She marvelled at the beautiful insect, and I admired its patience. It gave her a great comfort at the time, and I couldn't help but feel its reassurance that all would be well, that we could do this. It did seem far too early in the year and much too cold for such an amazing visitor. The butterfly had come to visit early that year, just for Gramma, because as the weeks slipped by, her light grew dimmer.

Grampy came to live with us in St. John's, where he thrived for almost two years with the wonderful support of Pam, his caregiver. Then, at eighty-nine, an infection sent Grampy to the hospital where he was diagnosed as being septic, quite the challenge for a man of his vintage. We took time off work in order to simplify the support and visits to the hospital. One evening, after six weeks had passed and I had spent the whole day at the hospital with him, I returned home sick with worry and fatigue. I sat on our front deck with a cup of tea, feeling completely overwhelmed, when a beautiful yellow and black butterfly came to share its calm energy with me. It glided once the length of the deck and then took flight, its visit just long enough for reassurance. We could do this . . .

The next evening I struggled with the decision to take extra time off work, decision-making not being my strong point. The following day was yet another day of keeping vigil over Grampy at St. Clare's Hospital. I was heading toward the driveway with homemade rhubarb jam and ice cream in tow when, approaching the car, came my guardian angel once again. Yes, the butterfly floated toward the driver's side of the car and over the bonnet, yellow and black in its glory. I knew then that I would be taking the extra time off work.

Life is too short not to listen to the special signs we are sent. Mine have always been inspirational; butterflies have been my guide.

Nobody knows what lies ahead of us in this life, but the endings are not always happy. Butterflies, though tiny and fragile, hold a secret. If you listen patiently, you'll hear their knowing whispers.

"He Was A Dream Maker"

NICOLE BEST

Noel's Pond, Newfoundland

As we stopped to take a big breath on the steps of the
First United Church on Park Street, the cold and sunny
day filled us with emotion. It was November 7, 2008,
the day that we would say our final goodbye to our
father, husband, poppy, and friend.

My father was a good man, and a loving man, as
well as a well-known businessman in Corner Brook.
His name was Allan Best, and at the tender age of
sixty-two, cancer had taken him too soon.

The church was filled with people wanting to pay
their last respects. It is a feeling that moves you
entirely, an experience that you only fully understand once you've experienced it. But that day, and
the recent days prior, I began to get a real under-
standing of how much my father really was loved.
You see, to us he was Dad, a man who loved his family and the beauty of the outdoors. He lived every
day with enthusiasm and enjoyed most of his time
with his wife of forty-two years and my mother,
Peggy, at their cabin in York Harbour.

Over the years, an appreciation grew for the kind
of man he was, the unforgettable jokes, and the lasting
smiles. But on that day, it had all come into perspec-
tive. As I listened to the words in his eulogy, I could

feel his strength. After the eulogy was read, my mother, my brother, and I were presented with the honour of receiving the Canadian flag. This flag was flown on the Peace Tower on Parliament Hill in Ottawa on November 4, 2008, the day of my father's passing. I knew my father would have been proud!

After we left the church, we learned of the power of butterflies. I knew we were not alone that day, and during the minister's prayers, a large black and yellow butterfly appeared in the church. The butterfly flew over all of the family members' heads, as if to circle us with strength. Then it pitched on the window, right in the middle of the pews. And there it stayed, giving comfort to all those who saw it.

When I think back of the odds of seeing a butterfly on a cold November day, I believe that the butterfly was there because of him, because of his strength, and because of his love. As someone said to us during that time, our father "wasn't a dreamer, he was a dream maker." He will be dearly missed. We love you, Dad, Al and Poppy.

Several months later, there was mention of my father in the local newspaper. As I read the article on butterflies, I again experienced an unusual occurrence, but this time the butterfly was transcribed on my arm. I have no idea how this happened. There was nothing there to aid in the ink's transfusion to my skin. As I looked down, temporarily tattooed to my arm was the wing of the butterfly, and as this was happening, my music box suddenly started to play its song. It was like his presence was with us again!

The following two stories were written about the same person. The first one was written by the niece of Vera Baars, and the second was written by her daughter.

Aunt Vera

CHERYL OLSEN

St. Catherine's, Ontario

In June 2003, after rushing my then nineteen-year-old son, Keith, to the hospital, he was diagnosed with a pinch in his urethra. Over the next five years and three urologists, he had a few major surgeries and numerous minor surgeries. Many nights I would talk to other family members that had previously passed away, asking that they help my son through all of this and help him to get well soon. He had to leave work in July 2009 to go on long-term disability, due to the severe pain and medications associated with his medical condition.

When my aunt, Vera Baars, was in the hospital, I would call her to see how she was, and her first question to me was always, "How is Keith doing?"

Aunt Vera passed away in 2008 of a brain tumour. Her daughter had made arrangements to have twelve Monarch Butterflies for release at her gravesite, and she asked Aunt Vera's two daughters, Joanne and Debbie, their children, my father, and Aunt Vera's closest friends to help release the butterflies. Aunt Vera had always loved Monarch

Butterflies and always had them in her backyard. After her funeral, I started asking for Aunt Vera's help with my son and his kidney condition. Within two weeks of talking to Aunt Vera almost every night, we finally got a date for my son to have his kidney removed. The surgery was held on December 5, 2008. He had a full recovery, with no more pain and no longer requiring medication.

In March 2009, my son applied to join the reserves with the Royal Canadian Armed Forces, something he had wanted to do since high school. All of the paperwork from his doctors had to be sent to Ottawa for medical clearance. It had been approximately three months and he had still not heard anything back. My son and I were sitting in the backyard one afternoon, and he was getting upset. I told him about talking to Aunt Vera almost every night, asking for her help prior to getting his kidney removed. We joked that it took a woman to get things going in the right direction. At that moment, a Monarch Butterfly flew down beside my son and perched on the barbecue next to him. I told him that it was Aunt Vera and that she was listening to us and telling us that he would hear back soon. Within days, my son heard from the army that his medical was cleared.

We had a family reunion on June 27, 2009, that we have every year, and this year it was held in honour of Aunt Vera at my parents' house in St. Catherine's, Ontario. My mom and dad had butterfly decorations all over their yard, and we talked about our memories of Aunt Vera. We all miss her, but every time we see a butterfly, we know she's close by.

She Loved Birds and Butterflies

JOANNE LINTHWAITE

Pickering, Ontario

My mother, Vera, passed away in September 2008 of a brain tumour. She had been living with my family and I, and had always loved birds and butterflies. We would sit out on our deck for endless hours watching for them to come. We had bird feeders and had a butterfly bush, and spotting them always gave us such joy.

Vera Baars was a loving grandmother and mother. In March of 2008, she had difficulty walking and was told she was suffering from a pinched nerve. By the end of March she was not able to move much of her left leg and arm, so we rushed her into the hospital, thinking she had had a stroke. Unfortunately, she was diagnosed with glyoblastoma, a cancerous brain tumour that was inoperable. My mom fought hard through the radiation treatments and continued her battle with every ounce of strength she had. My mom was not only my mother, but my best friend as well. We did almost everything together. She lost her battle on September 25, 2008.

In her honour, I held a butterfly release at her graveside service. She would have loved it. It was a rainy day, but just before the graveside service, the sun came out and we were able to do the butterfly release. Some of the butterflies did not come awake at first, and we put them on the numerous bouquets of flowers in hopes that, with the sun, they would awaken. The service was beautiful.

The next day I returned to the grave to have some private time with my mom and tell her how much I already missed her and loved her. I asked her, if it was possible, to please give me some kind of a sign if she was okay and happy. Of course, nothing happened, until I was almost back to my car. I had caught something, out of the corner of my eye, and turned my head to see the most beautiful Monarch Butterfly sitting on my left shoulder. It sat there for a minute or two, then gently lifted up, swirled around my head and legs before it lifted off up into the sky. I was crying so hard, as I am now, just thinking of that wonderful event. Coincidence, maybe, but I believe in my heart that it was my mom telling me she will always be looking out for me and will be sitting on my shoulder for the rest of my life.

Since then, butterflies have come and gone in my life, at times when I most needed to feel her. My son had surgery on a broken finger in July 2009. At the hospital, they asked us to pick a bed (it was a ward room of four beds) for him to get comfortable and wait for his surgery. We picked the bed in the corner, for no particular reason. Once my son sat down on the bed we realized why—on the ceiling above the bed was a painted collage of Monarch Butterflies. We both looked at each other and said, "Gramma is watching out for us. She is always here." I know that my mom is always with us, and the butterflies keep coming back to prove it!

The following story is one that has a message for someone who is ill but there is no death involved. The butterfly brings a message of hope.

"You're Staying Here With Us"

JACKIE FOLLETT

St. John's, Newfoundland

This is actually a happy story of hope and life. Four years ago, my younger sister, Joanne, had been diagnosed with aggressive ovarian cancer. She was thirty-nine years old, a wife, and the mother of two young children, aged seven and nine. I wondered how this could be happening, as we had lost our brother just over a year and a half ago. Our family was devastated and terrified, but we wouldn't even discuss the possibility of her dying, even though I know it was in all of our thoughts.

It had been a beautiful sunny day at Joanne's summer home in Cull's Harbour. We were outside on her pool deck admiring her flowers and discussing life. She had confided in me with some of her thoughts and feelings that I knew she hadn't discussed with anyone else. She was in the middle of her chemotherapy treatments, and all of her hair was gone. It was warm and she said, "Would it bother you if I took off my scarf?" I remember looking at her and feeling this ache in my heart, and a hollow, sick feeling in my stomach. She looked so frail and sick and I couldn't do anything to help ease her pain.

80

We were standing over a flower box on the rail of the deck, which was about chest high. The flowers were so full of life. A beautiful Monarch Butterfly landed between us on one of the flowers. It was so close we could see it as if it were magnified. I said, "Joanne, my friend Sally told me when she sees a butterfly she believes it is her mom sending her a message from Heaven." We didn't speak and the butterfly stayed between us for what seemed a very long time. It was the most amazing thing. I just felt this feeling come over me that I can't explain, and I looked at her and said, "This butterfly is here to tell us that you aren't going anywhere, and you're staying here with us just like the butterfly." I think we both felt something that day that will stay with us forever.

I am very happy to say, four years later, that Joanne is healthy and cancer-free. We both give each other, and the special people in our lives give, butterfly gifts whenever we can, as they now hold a special place in both of our hearts.

This is another Butterfly Messenger story that does not involve death, but rather it has to do with butterflies that appear after a loved one has left to return home from a visit. The butterfly brings a message of reassurance that the travelling person is safe.

Comforting and Reassuring

MORGANN TOMLINSON

Edmonton, Alberta

I was born and raised in Northern Ontario and now live in Edmonton, Alberta, with my young family. Every time I go back home to visit my mom, dad, and two sisters, which is usually once a year, we seem to see an alarming number of butterflies. It usually amounts to ten to twenty sightings every day. Maybe it's the same one each time, but one seems to be always hovering around us. We are usually at the lake and we spend a lot of time outside. All during my visit, and a day or two after I leave, this butterfly lurks around my mother's house. This has been happening for almost ten years now.

Often, my mother is upset when I leave and, when she sees the butterfly, she thinks of me and it makes her feel better. On one occasion a butterfly landed on her shoulder as she stepped out of the airport terminal after watching me leave on my flight. On another occasion a butterfly was inside my sister's house when she got home after saying goodbye to me at the airport.

I find it strange that these butterflies show up when I'm there and stay after I go back home, but only for a little while. I wonder if the butterfly is just comforting us and reassuring us, and letting us know we will see each other again.

A Message of Hope

BLAIR (WARREN) WHEELER

I received a sign of comfort from a butterfly during a recent difficult time. I was at Western Memorial Regional Hospital for two weeks following a car accident that I just barely survived. I crawled out of the wreckage with broken bones protruding out of my leg, a cracked sternum, and a broken back. My wife, Theresa, suffered similar injuries. We were both able to get out just before the vehicle became engulfed in flames and exploded. The doctors were baffled that I was able to crawl through the window and for her to get out through her door, which was partially blocked. We both had thought we were going to die, but I guess it just wasn't our time. One day in the hospital ward, where I was bedridden for those long, hard days of recovery, I was looking out the window, which I often did, and saw a beautiful big butterfly fluttering around. I remember thinking how odd it was, as the window was three storeys up from ground level, and not a height at which you'd expect to see a butterfly. It was the only sign of life I had seen outside that window the whole time—not a fly or a moth or anything, just that one lone butterfly. Maybe it was someone sending me a message.

"I'm Not Afraid of Dying"

LYDIA HISCOCK

Conception Bay South, Newfoundland

One of my hobbies in my younger days was a small flower business with annuals, perennials, and some old-fashioned varieties. Almost every season I would import a different kind of flower to add variety to the regular bouquet baskets. This particular year, the flowers I imported had a surprise that I never saw before. When the flowers started to bloom, there were patches of white butterflies all around the soil as well as around the flowers. There were very small ones and some a bit larger, and they were all white. Some couldn't use their wings, which were very tiny, but they grew really fast and each day their appearance changed. In one patch there seemed to be less white ones, but a new colour— blue with gold spots. Then there were no white ones at all, but all different colours in every patch. This happened in every patch, and then, after they changed colours, they would disappear. There were blue, green, yellow and gold. The last were a couple of large brown ones with gold spots. There were a lot of questions left unanswered. How did they get in my flower bed? It had never happened before! Were there eggs or caterpillars in the flowers? Did one butterfly produce all the butterflies of different colours, or did one butterfly produce all the butterflies of the same colour? I never did find out. That was my first encounter with butterflies, and they gave me great pleasure.

My next encounter was very different and left my family and myself with long-lasting memories that were also very sad. Our daughter, Judy, had just finished high school when she went to work at the university as a mail clerk. Over the years she worked her way up to a managerial position, a position she held until her retirement at age fifty-five. She had lots of plans for her retirement—she wanted to spend more time with her husband and two children, and to spend more time at their cabin and in her garden. However, God had other plans for her. Six months after her retirement, after several trips to her doctor and the hospital, she was told she had an incurable cancer. It was a huge shock to everyone. When I was visiting her in the hospital one day, I asked her how she felt about dying. She said slowly, "I'm not afraid of dying, I've been ready for a long time." That was the last time I spoke to her; she died a few days later.

Her funeral was held at the Salvation Army Citadel, with Lieutenant Colonel Ralph Stanley officiating. It was a beautiful sunny day in June, with a very slight breeze blowing. Judy's brothers, sisters, and immediate family and I were sitting in the front pew. I was sitting on the end, opposite the back window. There was a faint knock on the window, but no sign of anyone or anything. As I watched, the window began to open, not suddenly, but slowly and very quietly. My eyes were glued to the open window, wondering how the window had opened on its own. As I continued to look in amazement at this unusual occurrence, something else caught my eye. I suddenly saw a huge brown, spotted butterfly, in the space created by the open window. It fluttered its wings a few times and then flew into the church, and flew within a few inches of the heads of the grieving family in the front pew. Then, in a perfectly straight line, as if it were on a mission, it flew to the coffin where my daughter's body lay. It hovered for a few moments over the coffin, and then gently settled itself in the centre facing Reverend Stanley, who was giving the eulogy. It was as though the butterfly was paying attention to him. After a few moments, the butterfly flew from the coffin and, retracing its flight, flew back out the open window, pausing for a second to flap its wings as though to say goodbye. The people in the church just stood in awe and could not believe what they had just witnessed. Perhaps the butterfly was saying goodbye to my daughter in a way that none of us had ever seen before.

Judy's daughter now has a little girl of her own. In a conversation with her this past summer, she told me that, when she and her little girl are outside in the summertime, if there are butterflies they always hover around her and the little girl; sometimes one will even land on her little girl's hand. She feels that the butterflies hovering around her are letting her know that her mother's spirit will be with her always and is watching over her and her granddaughter.

"You Will Know"

RUBY PALMER

Toronto, Ontario

I recently asked my son if he remembered what I had told him about the butterfly that I had seen at my workplace one morning about a year ago. He told me that he remembered very well. That day was July 4, 2008. It was the anniversary of the day that my best friend had died ten years before.

I met my friend in 1980, at my workplace at the time. I started working there three months after she did. We became such good friends that we were like sisters. She would babysit my son when I wanted to go out with my boyfriend, whom I actually met through her. We were friends for eighteen years, and my son loved her like an aunt and always called her Auntie Mona. Her son and her brothers would visit us, and we would visit them. Mona was such a good person, and we had so much fun going on picnics together. My boyfriend and his parents had known her long before I knew her. Many, many times she would tell me, "If I should pass on before you, I will send you a sign every now and then." My son asked her how we would know if it was her, and she replied, "You will know."

Mona knew that I loved butterflies. I visited Tennessee in 1981, and brought her back a butterfly that I found on a flower in front of the Graceland mansion. It was already dead, so I put it in a plastic bag and gave it to her when I came home. After that, she said that I always reminded her of a butterfly. She would always tell me how proud she was to know me, because I always tried to help people, and she told me that she had never met anyone like me.

Mona died on July 4, 1999. Every year, my son and I remember that day. In 2008, on July 4, I went to work in the morning not thinking about what day it was at the time. I was working as usual when, all of a sudden, I saw a big, beautiful butterfly flying around me. The butterfly flew over to the next table, where my boyfriend was working. I said to him,' "Look, there's a butterfly!" It was a big brown and orange butterfly. I had never seen a butterfly of any kind flying inside my workplace before. Then, just like that, I suddenly remembered what day it was. I was so shocked and surprised about what I had just realized that I could barely speak. I said to my boyfriend, "Do you know what day this is? This is the day that Mona died ten years ago!" I asked my boyfriend if he thought the butterfly was Mona, coming back to remind me of what day it was. What was even stranger was that, after I told him that I remembered what day it was, the butterfly disappeared.

My boyfriend and I looked all around the room for the butterfly. We asked everyone if they had seen a big brown and orange butterfly. Everyone said that they hadn't seen a butterfly anywhere that day. When I got home that evening, I told my son what happened and he said that he believed that it could have been a message from Mona. I never could make up my mind if it was Mona or not, but my son and I now both believe that it was her coming to visit that day.

"Goodbye, See You Soon"

WENDY HAIGH

Mount Pearl, Newfoundland

I have a special connection with butterflies, blue butterflies in particular. You see, nine years ago, in May of 1999, I was pregnant with our little boy, Kaylin. When I went for my eight-month checkup, they told me that he had passed away. Needless to say, that day and the week that followed were very traumatic for my husband and me and our families. I was comforted by a minister while having Kaylin in the hospital and thought a lot of this lady, so much so that we asked her to perform the graveside service for our little boy.

It was a hot summer day in Toronto when we buried Kaylin, and all of us—friends and family, as well as family that had come from Newfoundland—were gathered around his little grave, saying prayers, recalling memories, and playing songs that I used to play for him in my tummy. I only remember certain moments of that day, but vividly remember seeing a rather large butterfly flying in and out around all of us, as if to say, "Hi, I am here!" At that time I did not make the connection; however, after the funeral, my mother-in-law had brunch at her house and the minister was sitting next to me. She remarked that she had also noticed the butterfly and began to enlighten me on the possibility of my little boy visiting and comforting me in the form of a most peaceful butterfly.

Shortly after that, I visited the cemetery with a friend of mine one afternoon and, while walking, we saw the blue butterfly. He landed about two feet from us, and when we approached, it seemed to fly another foot or so ahead, as if playing. I thought, *Gee, my little boy is playing with me!* After doing this a few times, he gently floated up, almost as if to say, "Goodbye, see you soon!"

My mother has also had butterfly moments that she believes to be her first grandchild visiting. Ever since that first sighting, I converse to my blue butterfly friends in whom I seek solace. I truly believe that my special little angel visits me in the form of a butterfly so I know that he is free and beautiful and is watching over my family and me.

I have since gotten a butterfly tattoo, as well as planted a butterfly garden and a butterfly bush—my way of saying thank you and to provide a place for him to rest whenever he wishes to drop in for a visit.

Monarch Place

ANN MARIE McGRATH

Dunville, Newfoundland

My dearest friend, Bonnie Friel, who lived in Laurel, Maryland, passed away October 26, 2005. She had been diagnosed with pancreatic cancer in September 2005. To say I was devastated is an understatement. She was buried at Arlington Cemetery in November (this was due to the fact that there is a waiting list for burials there, as her husband, David, was ex-military). We went to the funeral there, and that very day when we returned to their home, a butterfly was following Bonnie's granddaughter, Ashlyn, and me in the garden. I did not pay any particular attention to it at the time, but I do remember her daughter saying that her grandmother was in our midst and that butterflies were very dear to her.

The following spring and over the summer during my regular daily walking, I would often encounter butterflies, usually Monarchs. I had not mentioned this to my husband, until he returned from our cabin and mentioned that he had seen butterflies out there on several occasions, and most especially on that particular day.

Then, in July of 2007, Bonnie's husband, David, and his sister came to visit us. This was his first visit to Newfoundland without Bonnie. We were very anxious about the initial meeting and knew it would be an emotional experience. About five minutes before Dave and his sister arrived, I went to the door as I thought I heard them coming. Lo and behold, there was a Monarch Butterfly pitched on the rail of the step. I'm sure it was Bonnie letting me know she was also visiting with them.

The next day we took David and his sister to Signal Hill for some sightseeing. After our visit, we went down to Water Street. We were all a little hungry, so I decided to go to a snack van and get some fries. I was there alone, waiting for my order, when David decided I needed help to bring the fries back to the vehicle. He came and stood beside me, and while we waited, a beautiful Monarch Butterfly pitched directly on a stack of napkins in front of us. He was just as blown away as I was, and then he proceeded to tell me how often he had seen butterflies when he visited Bonnie's grave at Arlington. To me, it was just too much of a coincidence.

Later that summer, my husband came home with a plaque with a nice engraving for our cabin. I wasn't aware, but he had named our cabin "Monarch Place" in honour of Bonnie. From my personal experiences, I think there is definitely quite a lot of truth that butterflies are messengers.

The Giant Chrysalis

CRYSTAL BARTLETT-BOWERS

Burlington, Newfoundland

Twenty-one years ago, when I was just twelve years old, my father passed away. Needless to say, I was devastated. At such a young age I had never experienced a feeling like that before, and I didn't know how to deal with such a tragedy. I felt as if my father was suffering out there somewhere and there was nothing I could do to help him. I became tormented with a helpless feeling inside me.

Shortly after my father's passing, I began to have a recurring dream that gave me the peace and comfort I needed to deal with everything. In the dream, I was walking down a dirt road with old greying buildings and wooden boardwalks lining both sides, kind of like in an old western scene. I walked to the end of the buildings and turned right, where there was another building, but it was recessed back farther than the others. In the corner, where the building joined onto the next, hung a large chrysalis. I stood there staring at it and in awe of its massive size, and wondered why on earth it was there in such a strange place. Then it began to move and, before my very eyes, my father stepped out, reborn. He very gently said to me, "You see, my love, I am fine. Don't worry about me; I will be all right." His eyes were so full of love. In the dream, I could literally feel myself breathe again, as if a great weight was lifted from my shoulders. He then turned and walked away ever so slowly, as if to give me a chance to make peace with it all, and to say goodbye.

I had that same dream every night for about a week, and every morning I woke up feeling a little more peaceful, and dealing with my father's death began to become a little more bearable. Since then, butterflies have always held a very special symbolism to me, as though each one holds a little piece of my father.

Tara's Butterfly

BETTY BECK

Cold Lake, Alberta

It was eighteen years ago on December 8 that our daughter, our beautiful little girl, Tara, who appeared to be a very healthy eight-and-a-half-year-old, suddenly became very ill. She was diagnosed with ALM, an adult form of leukemia which is not very common. The prognosis was not good, but she had the most positive attitude throughout her treatments and procedures, of which there were many.

As a small child, Tara had loved butterflies and rainbows. After eighteen months of treatments and a cancelled bone-marrow transplant, the end of such a beautiful, vibrant physical life was in sight. I should add that Tara was very active in our church, St. John the Evangelist in Topsail, and had a great faith for someone so young. One day about two weeks before her death, she was sound asleep and a beautiful smile appeared on her face, like she was enlightened. When she woke, she said, "Mom, I had the most wonderful dream. I dreamed that I died and went to Heaven and came back as a beautiful butterfly and you put me in a jar and kept me forever."

I was so glad that there were others in the room to witness this. After the dream, all she wanted to do was cuddle until the end of her time. She talked quite freely about her death, so we shared her butterfly story with family and friends. Over the years we have had many butterfly stories of our own.

On the day that Tara had her dream, one of our family members had a butterfly fly very close to her face inside a tunnel at Memorial University. My sister saw a butterfly on her window on her birthday in April. Another time, as we renovated my grandfather's house, a butterfly was with us most of the time, usually landing on Tara's brother.

Many people have told us that if they were having a bad day and a butterfly came by, they think of Tara and they have a feeling of peace. It seems as though butterflies surround us whenever we need a little something extra. In Tara's honour, there is a butterfly stained glass window in our church. At her school, there is a website with a butterfly theme, and at the Janeway Hospital there is a butterfly clock made by someone in Ontario that we have never even met.

The story goes on and on after all these years. My husband died five years ago, and a beautiful butterfly bush was planted in the "Garden of Hope" in his memory. We now usually see two butterflies together!

My interpretation of Tara's dream: the butterfly in the jar is Tara, who is in my heart forever. It gives me peace! "What the caterpillar calls the end of the world, the Master calls a butterfly!"

My Mother Was Close By

LINDA WHIFFEN

Fox Harbour, Newfoundland

My mother, Elizabeth Stockley, who was a great believer in dreams and omens, passed away on August 12, 2009. A friend of hers, Jean Rumboldt, who was at her funeral, told us that when someone dies, you begin to see butterflies more frequently. I didn't pay much attention to this until the morning of my mom's funeral. My sister and I were out on my brother's patio in the Codroy Valley. It was a beautiful day, and we happened to notice three beautiful yellow butterflies fluttering around. Immediately, the story that had been told to me by Jean flashed into my mind, and I felt that my mother was close by. It was amazing!

A few days after the funeral, my sister-in-law and I were driving across the island to my mother's home in Fox Harbour. We stopped at the Irving restaurant in Grand Falls for lunch. After finishing, we were walking out through the door, and suddenly a beautiful red and black butterfly flew around me, down around my legs. I remarked to my sister-in-law, "There's Mom, making sure we are going to have a safe trip back." I had no doubt that my mom was with us that day.

"On A Wing and A Prayer"

MARILEE PITTMAN

Corner Brook, Newfoundland

My ex-husband and I maintained a very close and loving relationship after we divorced. We continued to celebrate Christmas and birthdays together as a family. He even continued to send me yellow roses for our anniversary, even though he often missed the actual day. Usually a bouquet would arrive at my home out of the blue with a "Happy Anniversary" card attached. If either of us went away on a trip we would call each other, and we always brought a little gift home for the other. We were lucky to have had a bond that had survived our divorce.

When he died at sixty-one, I felt cheated. He had so much more living and loving left to do. His two precious daughters were devastated. He had been their North Star. He would never get to know his grandchildren, nor would they ever experience first-hand their remarkable grandfather. Almost a year to the day after he died, our youngest daughter got married at my cabin. As I walked her up the path through the woods to a point overlooking the beautiful Bay of Islands, a brown butterfly followed us. We jokingly said that it was her father, coming to watch her get married. It became an inside joke that whenever something special was happening, a brown butterfly would appear.

We would say, "Oh, there's Dad!" It seemed to always happen out of the blue. This has been happening for the past eight years.

This past spring, I took my dog for a walk along a trail behind the old hospital. I looked up at what I thought was a dead leaf hanging off a branch. I thought to myself, *How odd that all of the other leaves blew off that tree and this one hung on through the winter.* Just then, the leaf blew away and I realized it was not a leaf at all, but a brown butterfly. I started to cry. I don't know why, but I knew it was my husband, and as I walked I pondered my grief and our relationship. I asked myself the question, "If I had to do it all over again, would I marry him?" I thought about the question for a while, then let it go unanswered. When I approached the place where I usually turn around, the brown butterfly brushed past my cheek so close I could feel its wings. I knew I had the answer to my question.

About a month ago, I was scheduled to do a workshop at a conference. When I arrived I discovered that another person was doing a workshop on the same topic as I had planned. Rather than have two workshops that were the same, I decided over the lunch break to change the topic of my workshop to conflict resolution. It was a subject I had some experience and training in; however, I had no materials. I really felt I was going on "a wing and a prayer." I knew I didn't want it to be too sombre, so I decided that I would try to make it creative and fun.

As the participants started to return to their seats, a brown butterfly entered the room. Some people looked a little annoyed, and in a panic I yelled out,

"Don't kill it, it's my husband!" With that I started the workshop and incorporated the beautiful butterfly into the program. While we discussed ways of resolving conflict in a healing way, the butterfly gently investigated the participants, landing on a hand or a shoulder. At one point it hid under a piece of paper. It seemed so calm and at home. It remained for almost the entire workshop, exiting as quietly as it had come when we broke into small groups.

Each group was directed to do a presentation. I had asked them not to be too serious in their reports and to use art, drama, or other creative means to present their thoughts. Every group incorporated the butterfly into their presentations. They spoke about feeling the fragility of the butterfly and the need to protect it from harm. They saw it as a spiritual symbol of transformation. Almost everyone present felt a personal connection to the butterfly through loss of a loved one. It seemed to symbolize the fragility and transient nature of life. It truly was an amazing experience. We spoke of it after as being a remarkable event that we felt privileged to have shared.

One might question what a butterfly has to do with conflict. It has to do with the gentleness we see in nature. It has to do with how we are presented with signs of a spiritual nature if we are open to receiving them. They point to a different way of dealing with difficulty, such as the end of a marriage. Love doesn't have to end with a death or divorce—it just may take on a different form . . . perhaps that of a brown butterfly!

"I'm Sure That's Noble"

DAVID AND VIOLET ROBERTS
Chevery, Quebec

We had gotten a Nova Scotia Duck Tolling Retriever for our three children when they were ages seven, eleven and fifteen. We called the dog Noble, and he was the highlight of our family. We each had a different relationship with the dog. Living in a small community of about 350 people, we didn't have a college or university, so as our children graduated from high school, one by one they left home to go off to school in Montreal. Of course, the bond with our dog became even more special.

This past summer when my husband and I started our summer vacation in July, we went to our cabin with Noble. We were only there a few days when we noticed he wasn't eating very much. A few days later he started vomiting at night.

In August, our daughter came home for a week's vacation. Three days after our daughter arrived home, on Sunday morning, Noble passed away. It was a very sad time for us, losing our dog that we had all cherished for fifteen and a half years.

A couple of days after Noble died, we took our daughter fishing on the river, a place where we had spent many fun-filled hours with our family and Noble on our summer vacations. While my husband was fishing for salmon, my daughter and I were sitting in the boat watching him, when along came a beautiful black and white butterfly. It circled around us a few times and then landed on the front seat, exactly where Noble had always sat. It then flew to the bottom of the boat and landed right in the dip net. I said to my daughter, "Oh my God, I'm sure that's Noble," because he was always sniffing the dip net or trying to lick the fish in the net. It stayed there for quite some time before flying off. My husband wasn't having much luck with fishing, so we decided to go farther upriver, where the butterfly appeared again, flying around us.

When we went back downriver and we were hauling our boat ashore, the same butterfly appeared yet again. I've never been a superstitious person, but I'm sure that was Noble's spirit, or a sign from someone very powerful.

Mom's Purple Butterfly

BARBARA LAWLOR

St. John's, Newfoundland

I want to share my story about a wonderful experience that occurred shortly after my mother's passing last Victoria Day weekend. By way of a little background, my mother passed away in March of 2009, at the age of eighty-eight years. During her last few years, she suffered extreme back pain from arthritis and was unable to get around without assistance. She often spoke about being tired of the pain and wanting to be with our dad, who had passed away five years previous. My response to her was always that God would take her in His own good time.

Mom loved butterflies and found it fascinating when they pitched on her, which happened quite often over the years. She also loved the colour purple, especially lighter shades such a mauve and lilac, and she wore these colours quite often. My mom had snow-white hair and a beautiful complexion.

A few years ago I took both of my parents on a bed and breakfast trip across Newfoundland, which included a visit to a butterfly conservatory that I had planned as a surprise. After her walk through the butterfly house, Mom happily perched herself on a bench where she remained for nearly two hours! I'm certain that each and every butterfly in the pavilion must have visited her. It was amazing!

One morning, about eight weeks after my mom's passing, my husband and I were walking along the beautiful boardwalk trail around Outside Pond in Winterton, where we were camping for the long week-end. It was a cool, clear morning and not the time of year one would see butterflies in Newfoundland. As we were walking along enjoying the solitude and quiet, a butterfly appeared about fifteen feet in front of us. It was a beautiful purple colour and quite large, about four to five inches across. We stopped walking and watched. It fluttered about in front of us for several seconds and moved forward only as we started forward again. I said, "Hi, Mom, how are you doing?" and commented to my dumbfounded husband that the appearance of the butterfly was Mom's way of letting us know she was no longer in pain and that she was finally at peace in Heaven with Dad. The butterfly eventually flew off over the pond through a wide opening in the trees. It was a joy to witness and it brought such peace to my mind that everything was okay.

"Is Everything Okay?"

ANN MARIE SUTHERLAND

Antigonish, Nova Scotia

In 1996, I was working as a teacher's aide in a grade-three class when circumstances arose and I decided to take a year's leave and move to Halifax. I had become quite attached to one bright girl in the class who seemed to be less fortunate than others but had amazing spirit. My own daughter was just a few years older.

Before we moved, I asked my daughter if she would mind going through all the clothes she had and box up anything she didn't want or didn't wear anymore. I casually packed some painted butterflies that once graced the walls of my daughter's bedroom, tucking them in haphazardly throughout the box. She had outgrown the butterflies, so I thought they might find a new home with this young girl. I called the little girl's mom first to make sure she wasn't offended by the donation, for it was something that I really and truly wanted to do.

A few days before leaving for Halifax, I decided to go out to their home myself instead of taking the box to school. I remember driving to their home, completely overwhelmed with their living conditions and, later on, with their story. As I brought the box in to a very eager young girl and her little sister, the two dived in right away, pulling out article after article, along with the occasional butterfly, which I had forgotten that I even packed. I noticed that the mother had started to get a bit choked up. She had grasped her hands and held them around her mouth as in disbelief. It wasn't quite the reaction I had expected. "Is everything okay?" I asked. "Turn around, behind you," she replied. I turned around to find a huge butterfly on the wall behind me, almost identical to the ones I had packed, only much larger. The butterfly was so close it seemed to be almost perched on my shoulder. The girl's mother had tears in her eyes and told me that the picture on the wall was her mother. She had passed away two years to the very day and told them she would always come back to them in the form of a butterfly. I didn't know what to say, but I felt an immediate connection to this family and had an overwhelming sense that my packing of these butterflies was obviously more than coincidence—there was something else at play here.

It wasn't until about a year and a half later that I really started thinking more about this incident and others like it. More often than we realize, coincidences happen all around us but we are too busy to even recognize or acknowledge that they even occur, much less search for their true meaning. Or maybe we start noticing them only when we are ready, open, and able to see them.

In looking back at the simple but beautiful butterfly story, I am touched by the hope it brings. During this family's struggle and my own personal upheaval, there was definitely another All-Knowing element at play. Be it Higher Consciousness or the realm of spirit, something outside of myself was definitely sending that family a message of hope through my actions that day.

If Only We Knew

HELEN DURDLE

Birchy Cove, Newfoundland

Messengers do not always come in the form of a live butterfly. I wasn't actually visited by a butterfly, but I did have my own experience and reassurance in the form of butterflies.

My brother was lost at sea on a stormy February night. We will never know the details of his final hours, and I am not sure if any comfort would be gained through knowing. I, however, needed some reassurance that through all of this he was now at peace.

I read an article in a local newspaper about "life's little miracles." One in particular was about a person asking God if her loved one was okay after they had passed away. She asked for a sign in the form of a butterfly. After seeing butterflies here and there, she still was not convinced, so she asked for a sign she could not ignore. A shower of Monarch Butterflies flew up around her in the most unlikely place. She was convinced!

I also needed a sign, so I asked for it. Sure, I also saw butterflies here and there. I began to notice them on printed paper, on clothing, and, strangely enough, on television every evening. But I still needed something more, and I asked for another sign, as all of this could be just me looking for a sign everywhere.

A few days later I received a beautiful butterfly

poster in the mail. I couldn't believe it! I was convinced this was my sign. I am sure many people have received this same poster, but still, many have not. I asked for a sign and I received it. When I think of my brother now, I think of butterflies, and every time I see a butterfly I think of him. All of this beauty that surrounds us surely must mean something. If only we knew!

The following two stories are not about butterflies but their close cousins, the moths. Both stories are about the same type of moth, the Cecropia, *one of the biggest moths found in Canada and truly a giant in the order* Lepidoptera.

"It's Like Roxanne is Here With Us"

KERRY MANON HENSTRIDGE
Fort McMurray, Alberta

Our sister-in-law, Roxanne Henstridge, died of cancer on July 18, 2002. She discovered the cancer in September 2001, and was only thirty years old when she lost her life.

Roxanne was a young woman with lots of wisdom. She was a teacher and loved working with children. Roxanne was nominated for the Alberta School Boards Association 1998 Edwin Parr teacher award. Out of 120 candidates, Roxanne placed third. The principal of the school remarked of Roxanne, "I have rarely come upon someone in their first year of teaching that is a natural-born teacher." Roxanne clearly enjoyed being with children, and children clearly enjoyed her as well. The parents felt their children were in safe hands under Roxanne's care. She always had a smile on her face and was always willing to help out. She never judged and she accepted everybody the way they were. Roxanne was a very humble, gentle, loving, caring and soft-spoken person. She always had good advice to share if you asked her. She respected others. She really made a difference in this world and had a bright future ahead of her, and this made it hard for everybody to accept what was happening to her. It was very difficult to see her going through such a terrible ordeal. As family, we felt so helpless. We couldn't do anything to take the pain away or stop her disease. We had no power and no control during the eleven months of suffering she endured.

The following year in May, the Relay for Life event was held in Fort McMurray, Alberta, and as a family we decided to participate to raise money in her memory. Roxanne's sister Rochelle, her brothers and sisters-in-law, and her nieces and nephews who lived in Fort McMurray were all part of the team. It was an emotional time. We were all still in the first stage of grieving, as it had not yet been a year since she passed.

The Relay for Life was held in a field behind a school and was a twelve-hour event. It was the family's first time participating in an event with the organization. All around the inside of the track were luminary candles. Each candle was placed in a paper bag displaying the name of a loved one. On the outside of the track field were more luminary candles printed with the words Hope For A Cure. It symbolized the reason why we were there.

As a team, we had to have a team member on the track at all times for twelve hours. We decided that two family members were going to participate every hour. As it began getting dark, all of the candles around the track were lit by a family member in memory or in honour of a loved one. The light from the candles helped to guide our way around the track throughout the night. It was very touching.

We took turns walking throughout the night. Around three in the morning, we were starting to get tired. The weather was cool and damp and during the night it had rained, but we remembered our Roxanne, as she, too, had been tired, yet had kept fighting to the end. So we kept on walking in her memory and grieved her at the same time. Rochelle had noticed throughout the night that a butterfly had landed on one of the luminary candles that displayed the word "Hope." Early in the morning while walking, she again saw the butterfly on a luminary candle on the other side of the track. It wasn't until she came closer that she realized it was Roxanne's luminary candle that the butterfly had landed on. Rochelle had wanted to pick up Roxanne's candle and bring it back to our campsite. It was around 6:00 a.m. She didn't know what to do. She wanted to keep her sister's luminary candle, but at the same time she did not want to disturb the butterfly. Rochelle decided to gently pick up the luminary, and to her astonishment, the butterfly stayed on the candle. She brought it over to the campsite. Everybody was amazed. We were all looking at the butterfly, taking pictures and attracting people from other campsites. They were coming to see the butterfly, which did not move from its perch. Rochelle was getting more and more concerned, as she wanted to bring her sister's candle home but did not want to disturb the butterfly. She left the candle at the campsite and we went back to walking around the track as everybody continued to be amazed at the butterfly.

The final lap to close the event was announced, and all team members were to be on the track. Someone had the idea to get the luminary candle with the butterfly for the last lap. Manon, Roxanne's sister-in-law, went to the campsite to retrieve the luminary candle and, to her great surprise, the butterfly was still there! She brought it back to the track with her and the whole team gathered together and walked with the

luminary, watching every movement the butterfly made as we walked our final lap. We could not believe our eyes at the sight of the butterfly struggling to hold onto the luminary bag, just like our Roxanne had struggled to hold onto her life.

When the lap was over, the butterfly was still sitting on the luminary candle. We put it on the ground and we started to pack our gear to go home. By then it was shortly after 7:00 a.m., and the event was being concluded as someone announced the amount of money all teams had raised together. Brian, Roxanne's brother-in-law, won a cellular phone, and on the box there was a picture of a butterfly. This seemed to confirm with certainty that Roxanne was truly there with us. We went back to the campsite to pick up our gear and go, and saw that the butterfly was still clinging to the luminary bag. We all surrounded it and just kept looking at it with astonishment. I can still remember someone remarking, "It's like Roxanne is here with us!" The butterfly finally dropped off the bag and onto the ground. We were circled around it, and when it didn't move for a while we thought that maybe it was hurt. Then it started slowly moving, did three little circles, and flew away. We all looked up and said goodbye to Roxanne again. We knew that she had been with us that night.

Since then, the sight of a butterfly has had a very special meaning to our family. Every butterfly we see reminds us of our beloved Roxanne. Roxanne, you have touched our lives so deeply. You are in our thoughts and always in our hearts. We love and miss you dearly.

Friendly Giant

CINDY (PYE) POWER

Carbonear, Newfoundland

In June 2009, my son, Adrian Pye, and I went on a vacation to Ontario with his grandparents, Gerald Sr. and Judy Pye. We left Carbonear on our way to the mainland, stopping at the butterfly conservatory to show four-year-old Adrian the butterflies that were exhibited there. Adrian had always been fascinated with butterflies and we all knew he would surely enjoy being up close to hundreds of butterflies. Entering the conservatory, we were all amazed by the number and variety of butterflies and their vibrant colours. Adrian was truly astounded by it, and the smile on his little face as we headed back to the car to continue our journey had assured me that this trip was going to be great.

The purpose of the trip to Ontario was to take Adrian to Canada's Wonderland, the Toronto Zoo, Niagara Falls, and Marineland. It was also a chance to show Adrian and myself where Adrian's father, Gerald F. Pye, was born and raised until he was seventeen years old, when his family moved back to Newfoundland. In August of 2006, at the age of thirty-four, Gerald had been diagnosed with a very rare form of brain tumour. Adrian was only twenty months old at the time. The cancer was very aggressive, and within eight months, Gerald died. During his last few weeks he made us promise him that we would take Adrian to Ontario to see and do all the things that he had wanted to do with his little son but would no longer be around to do.

On our way to Ontario, we stopped in Scoudoc, New Brunswick, to visit with one of Gerald's aunts and her family. Gerald had always spoken highly of his Aunt Gail and her children. He even lived with them at one time, when he got his first real job away from home.

Adrian and I were outside playing at Gail's house when I noticed something in the tall grass around the oil tank. I went over to see what was there, and I had to push the grass away to get a better look. I could hardly believe my eyes when I saw it. It was the biggest and most beautiful butterfly I had ever seen. It was simply huge. I first thought it was a plastic decoration put into the ground. I couldn't believe it was real until I saw its wings gently move. I called Adrian over and we gathered the rest of the family members to come see it for themselves. The butterfly was so tame that I was able to pick it up and place it in my son's hand, to have some photos taken of him with the beautiful creature. The butterfly's wingspan was the width of Adrian's forearm and its body bigger than my thumb. The butterfly stayed on Adrian's arm for at least ten minutes and was not afraid of us at all. It was as if it was trying to be close to us, or trying to tell us something. There was such a feeling of peace among us all and we felt what was surely Gerald's presence at that time. Adrian, so unaware of the magnitude of what we were all feeling and thinking, was still in awe of what he just experienced.

After the encounter, Gerald's parents and I strongly believe that Gerald was there with us in spirit, in the form of a big beautiful butterfly, on our trip to Ontario. We knew from this experience that he was happy that we were keeping our promise to him by taking Adrian on this journey. On the trip we were given a book on butterflies and moths and we discovered that what we saw was called a Giant Silkworm Moth, or *Cecropia*, and that it is native to North America. This family of moths contains the largest and most beautiful insects in the world.

For anyone who had the fortunate opportunity to meet my husband, Gerald Pye, they would all describe him as a "friendly giant." He was a beautiful person in every way. Therefore, I believe that this beautiful giant moth was Gerald, letting us know that he will always be with us.

ADRIAN PYE

Aubrey Was With Us Again

GAIL PIKE

Goose Bay, Labrador

My husband, Aubrey, passed away seven years ago. Soon after he died, my daughter came for a visit. It was October in Labrador, not a time you would expect to see butterflies. She was standing on the patio one day when a beautiful butterfly landed on her shoulder. She said she believed it was her dad coming to visit her. She told me that wherever she goes, butterflies always seem to follow her. I was more than skeptical at her claim.

A couple of years later, while I was attending a Mothers Against Drunk Drivers conference, we were each given a beautiful Monarch Butterfly to set free in remembrance of loved ones we have lost. There were about 200 people there, and all were given a butterfly to release. Upon the release, my butterfly refused to fly away. I tried unsuccessfully to get it to fly, but it always came back and landed on my shoulder. As it was getting close to our time to leave, I decided to take the butterfly with me. I placed it in a box and took it to my girlfriend's house, where I was going to stay for a few days.

My friend has a beautiful garden, and it was there that we decided to set the butterfly free. It continued to stay around the garden. In the morning we would have coffee on the patio and my butterfly would flutter around us. We joked that Aubrey was with us again. I stayed for four days, and the butterfly was there the entire time. When I left, so did the butterfly. From that day on, I've seen butterflies all the time and feel a sense of comfort because I know that my husband is always with me.

Enjoying the Service

MAXINE DAWE

St. John's, Newfoundland

My husband, Bill, loved black butterflies. Soon after he died, the Wesley Men's Choir, of which Bill was a member, was invited to sing at the United Church in Botwood. The wives of the choir members went on the trip as well, so I decided to accompany them.

The service took place on a warm summer's day. All of the windows in the church were open. While the choir was singing, a large black butterfly flew into the church. It circled twice around the pew where I was seated, around the choir, and then situated itself on the organ for the rest of the performance. The organist happened to be one of Bill's best friends.

After the service, the minister apologized for the distraction by the butterfly. I told him that it was a comfort to me and that I felt that my late husband was sending me a message. He was enjoying the service and assuring me that all was well with him.

In the six years since Bill's death, I have received such reassurance many other times. At the cabin when I have troubles with the plumbing or run into other difficulties, a black butterfly will appear on the deck. On one occasion when a friend was giving me some bad news about his health, a black butterfly suddenly appeared on the door outside the cabin where we were standing. I hope the stories of my Butterfly Messenger will bring comfort to others just as butterflies have for me countless times over.

The April Visitor

GERRI BISHOP

Heart's Delight, Newfoundland

My daughters and I have had quite a few amazing experiences that have been a real inspiration to all of us in our time of sorrow and grief. At 4:10 a.m. on April 27, 2006, my husband, Sol, passed away suddenly of an aortic aneurism, which wasn't detected until an autopsy was performed. That night, two of our daughters returned home from Lloydminster, Alberta. Our other daughter, who lives in St. John's, also came home. They were all here along with the rest of the family that night, and everybody was in great shock.

The following morning when we all got up, our oldest daughter asked for a sign from her dad, to let us know that he was okay and that we would be all right. The morning was so beautiful, warm and sunny, just the way Sol had always loved. We all went outside to the backyard in our nightgowns to enjoy the sun and to hope and pray that what happened the day before was just a dream, but no such luck, it had happened. As we were all sitting and standing around, along came our sign that everything was going to be fine. A beautiful orange and black butterfly came fluttering around us. It stayed around us for what seemed like hours.We knew it was Sol there with us. Before it flew away that day, it flew up to our bedroom window, as if to look in and say goodbye. For the next three days, that butterfly would visit our backyard and spend time with us. We thought about how amazing it was to have a butterfly spending time with us in the month of April, but we all believed in signs from above and considered this to be ours. It gave us such great comfort in our time of sorrow and grief, and it helped get us through those three very difficult days and the many more that followed.

We really missed the visits from the butterfly after that Sunday, the day of the funeral. We didn't see another until sometime in June, the usual time for the butterflies to be seen. Then in July, my granddaughter, who was sixteen at the time, was in Alberta with her parents. One particular weekend, they went on a camping trip. They were at a lake for some sun and swimming, when an orange and black butterfly came and landed on my granddaughter's foot. She was so excited about this that she could hardly control herself. Her mom left the lake and went to their campsite to get her camera. Lo and behold, when she got back, the butterfly was still in the same place. She took several pictures, and it was so amazing. The butterfly remained close by all that afternoon. They said that when they went back to their campsite they swore that the same butterfly had followed them back there. They went back home that evening. My son-in-law was out on the patio barbecuing supper, when my daughter heard him shout for her to come out. She could hardly believe her eyes when she saw the butterfly there again. They had such a feeling of Sol's presence that day that it was incredible.

My husband and I always marvelled at butterflies.

We both loved to see and watch them flutter about every summer. When our oldest daughter, Tracy, got married in 1998, she and her dad danced to *Butterfly Kisses*. In 2001, we built a new house. Our oldest granddaughter lived with us, and when it came time to paint her bedroom, she wanted a blue room with butterflies. So I bought some decals, and she has a bedroom full of butterflies. I don't think that bedroom will ever be changed.

Butterflies have always had a special place in our hearts, but never as much as they have in the past three and a half years. My house is full of butterfly items and my family and friends are always giving me things with butterflies on them. I have vases, placemats, suncatchers, wall hangings, wind chimes—and the list goes on.

Just a couple of weeks ago, I went to Carbonear. It was a very cold and rainy day, and I had been having a really bad day. I was missing Sol so much that it hurt. I had to go to a garage to get the tire pressure checked on my Jeep. While the attendant was checking the tires, I noticed something moving inside a broken lens of the park light on the front of the Jeep. When I investigated further, there was a butterfly inside the lens. I picked it up in my hand and it was still alive, so I brought it home with me and put it in a flowerpot on my patio. The next morning, I checked on it, but it had died overnight. It now sits on my kitchen window. That incident brightened up my day so much; it was as if Sol was telling me that things would be just fine. One September, when there were no more butterflies, I found myself missing seeing them around. I wanted to do something to keep them around me all the time, so I decided to get a tattoo. I was in Alberta with my three daughters and my granddaughter at the time, and we all went to a tattoo parlour and got our butterflies for life! I got mine first, and placed it close to my heart. I had never wanted a tattoo until these comforting butterfly experiences started and continued, reminding me of Sol. It's been such an amazing inspiration to myself as well as my whole family. I tell everybody about our experiences. Most are really intrigued, while others just listen in disbelief. I really do believe we got the sign we needed that everything will be fine, and I know now that Sol will always be with us and is always watching out for us.

Wouldn't Miss This Day
for the World

LORI GALLO

Hamilton, Ontario

There are a couple of reasons why I believe in Butterfly Messengers. The first is that in the world in which we live today, we really need to believe in something so positive and inspiring to make the passing of our loved ones a little more bearable. Secondly, I believe because it actually happened to me two years ago, while planning my wedding.

After years of being together, Tony and I decided to make our union official. We chose to get married on a tour boat that runs out of Hamilton Harbour. We consulted with the manager on a couple of dates, ones I had chosen because my oldest sister, Marlene, would be visiting from home. The only date that was still available was Friday, August 31. This date was bittersweet as it was the birthday of our late sister, Cindy, who had passed on two years before. After giving it some thought, we decided that there was no better way to remember Cindy than to share our special day with her.

As the planning for the wedding continued, I noticed that my late mom and dad were on my mind a lot more. I also seemed to be having more frequent encounters with butterflies. On the Wednesday before the wedding, I went to consult with the manager of the tour boat for the last-minute details for the wedding. While leaving my house to go to the car, a Monarch Butterfly fluttered around me, almost playfully. Not really giving it much thought, I continued the drive to my destination. While walking toward the office I notice another butterfly, this one seeming to follow me as I walked.

The next day, more people arrived at the house in preparation for the big day, including my niece, my nephew, and his girlfriend, and another niece, the daughter of my deceased sister. We were outside in the backyard talking about my parents and sister Cindy and remembering the good times at my grandparents' and Cindy's houses. "Too bad they couldn't be here," someone remarked sadly. "Oh, they wouldn't miss this day for the world," I replied. "In fact, they have been with me all week, and are here with us right now!" Everyone looked at me as if I had lost my mind. Aunt Lori asked, "What in the world are you talking about?" But I just smiled and looked toward the sky. Everyone raised his eyes to see three butterflies fluttering around the house. I went on to explain the story of a loved one sending you a butterfly when you need a sign from someone you're missing. By the time I finished the story, they were all covered in goosebumps, awestruck, and a little teary-eyed. And now, they believe too!

On the morning of the wedding, I went outside to have tea and decided to talk to my missed family members. I told them that I'm fine, but asked them to please give me the courage to get through the day without them being there with me. Suddenly, a butterfly appeared, seeming to have come out of nowhere, and fluttered around my head before disappearing just as quickly as it had come. I laughed to myself and thanked the three of them for watching over me. I never saw another butterfly that day, but my wedding was wonderful.

Thanks Mom, Dad, and Cindy. I love you always and I miss you more today than I did on those horrible days when I heard you had left forever.

A Beautiful Butterfly

GERRY McDONALD

St. John's, Newfoundland

Sometimes we cling to anything that might give us the feeling of the presence of a loved one who has passed away. My wife, Ann, and I had four girls: Sheri, Lesley, Tia, and Vicky. Early in 2001, Ann and Lesley were both diagnosed with breast cancer. Lesley passed away on December 4, 2006, and Ann still fights on. Anyone who knew Lesley was aware that she loved butterflies.

In October of 2009, we had a storm with incredibly high winds on the Avalon Peninsula. During the storm, a ten-foot-long piece of metal fascia became dislodged from behind the gutter and was flapping like mad in the wind. At about five o'clock in the morning, not being able to put up a ladder, I managed to tie it onto the house until the winds died down. Later that day our son-in-law, Leo Ryan (Lesley's husband), came over to give me a hand.

As he proceeded to tack the fascia back in place he said, "Gerry, your gutter is blocked with leaves." He started to scoop out the leaves and I heard him say, "Wow, what a nice butterfly!" It was in amongst the leaves with its wings closed up. "I think it's gone," he said, indicating that he thought the butterfly was dead. He laid it on the roof and continued cleaning out the rest of the gutter, but lo and behold, it fell back in the leaves. He gently took it out again and said, "Lesley would have loved that one."

He placed it in my left palm, which was covered with a work glove. Its wings were still closed, but as I admired it, the wings began to slowly open to reveal its beautiful colours of yellow, brown, orange, and red. Almost as if it was teasing me, it closed its wings again, and it stayed in my hand as I made quick steps to the house to show the others inside. I held my right hand in front of my left to stop any wind from lifting it away. Inside, everyone was amazed. Ann, Tia, and her fiancé, Trevor, Vicky and her husband, Steve, and our sixteen-year-old granddaughter, Kayla, visiting from Nova Scotia, were all mesmerized by the beautiful creature.

The butterfly stayed in my hand and made little movements from left to right. Then, all of a sudden, it took flight and flitted around the living room. Every time it would land, Kayla would snap some pictures. Finally, it ended up in the venetian blinds, and every-one was scurrying to find it while I went back outside to give Leo a hand.

About ten minutes later, I was rounding the house in the back garden when I noticed Kayla standing with the patio door opened and releasing the butterfly from her hands. I watched it as it flew toward the shed and then into the maple tree. I looked and looked, but it was gone. Nobody said anything, but I think we were all having the same thoughts that day, that Lesley had paid us a visit in the form of one of her favourite things—a beautiful butterfly.

"I'll See You Later On Today"

GLYNN BISHOP

Paradise, Newfoundland

Mourning Cloaks (*Nymphalis antiopa*) vary greatly in size and colour. The word "butterfly" in Greek is psyche, which means "soul." The Irish saw butterflies as souls waiting to pass into purgatory. They were also symbols of rebirth after death and likened to the wandering consciousness during the dream state. They teach us grace and perseverance.

The day my father died, a Mourning Cloak Butterfly attached itself to the rock I was moving as I was constructing a rock wall in my garden. Just minutes later my sister called and told me he had just died. That was September 3, and throughout that week it had seemed as if Mourning Cloak Butterflies were always around. On October 16, I noticed that a Mourning Cloak butterfly had landed on the inside wall of my woodshed. When I stored my wood it did not move, and I was careful not to touch or move it as I stacked the wood. Bernard Jackson, a butterfly expert and former director of the Oxen Pond Botanical Garden, said that it was exceedingly rare to observe a butterfly at this time of the year, as it was overwintering. I was honoured! In mid-winter my friend and I photographed it for him. At -22° Celsius, the beads of condensation on its body were tiny spheres.

April 16 was the first nice warm day of that spring and the day the butterfly flew away. I looked one day, and it was gone. I saw a squirrel around that day and didn't know if Dad's butterfly had ended up as a surprise treat for it. I thought at that time it seemed coincidental to have all those Mourning Cloak events that year. I truly wondered if it could be true . . . that somehow Dad's spirit had enveloped a butterfly.

The day my mother was buried was a warm spring day, when all the days before were wet, windy and cold. The funeral was at 2:00 p.m., so I decided to go on a bicycle ride on the trails around Octagon Pond and Neil's Pond in Paradise. Where the trail meets the old track is a good place to rest for a moment.

As I came to a stop and put my foot on the ground, a large Mourning Cloak Butterfly flew up from under a bush and proceeded to fly all around me, touching and bumping into me all over. It travelled from my hat to my feet for several minutes, finally landing just above my knee. I said, "I'll see you later on today," and the butterfly flew away. My father was an alcoholic most of his life, and Mom endured many a hard night and day because of this. Toward the end of his life, Dad expressed regret over all the difficulties his drinking had caused. Of seven children, I was the most like him. I use to help him build boats when I was young, but as I grew older and tried to build my own boat, I had no help, only ridicule, from him. I think he came to me that day, in the form of the butterfly, to be near me and as some form of apology, a way of saying he was sorry for the lost opportunities for friendship.

Zachary's Place

KAREN COULTAS

St. John's, Newfoundland

My son Zachary Michael Strong was born October 21, 2000. He became an angel on September 17, 2007. That year, he had been anxiously awaiting his seventh birthday. September 17 was a beautiful and warm sunny Monday. Zachary was riding his bicycle, on his way to the playground just down the street from where we were living, in Airport Heights, St. John's. He rode out into the path of an oncoming dump truck and, as I was told, was killed instantly. That day, our world fell apart, and we were left trying to understand, trying to pick up the pieces, and wondering how to explain to our three-year-old son why his brother never came home from the park.

It is because of all the bereaved parents I met online, and with the help of some books I purchased, that I learned of signs—of what to look for, and of what to ask for.

In 2008, the last week of March, I found myself in a state that had become quite common for me—crying, and desperately wishing to have my son here, or to know that he was safe. I asked Zachary if he would please send me a butterfly, to let me know he was okay, that he was with me, that he could hear me. Almost immediately, I realized how foolish my request was, and how impossible. The odds of seeing a butterfly in Newfoundland in March—well, I figured they must be astronomical. I was driving at the time, on my way to visit my mother in Portugal Cove. I arrived at her house upset and agitated, and was about to tell her of my silly request, when a butterfly came flying right over the roof of the house and flew a circle around us twice. Then, just as fast, it was gone again. Needless to say, that day changed everything for me. I knew Zachary had granted me my sign and had sent the butterfly to me. I became a believer.

Zachary's school, Roncalli Elementary, did a butterfly release at the park at the end of the 2007–2008 school year. The park was renamed in memory of my son and is now called "Zachary's Place." I got to hold a butterfly in my hand that day, and it was a moment I will never forget.

ZACHARY MICHAEL STRONG

While I was working on Butterfly Messengers, *I received the following addition to Karen's story. It is one of the most remarkable stories I have ever received.*

The Best Christmas Gift

KAREN COULTAS

St. John's, Newfoundland

My mother got up on Christmas Eve morning, December 24, 2009, and, just like every other morning, her first thoughts were of her grandson Zachary and how much she missed him. But just like every other morning, she got up to face the day ahead.

As she came downstairs in her house, she stopped in the living room, plugged in the Christmas tree, and went to the kitchen to fix a cup of tea for herself and my father. As she walked over to the fridge to get a tin of milk, something caught her eye. There, sitting on the door of the fridge, was a small brown butterfly with blue flecks. As you can imagine, she thought she was seeing things, but grabbed her digital camera right away. My mom took several pictures of the butterfly, and also some of the Christmas decorations, to prove it really was Christmas Eve. She was so afraid we would not believe it!

A butterfly in Newfoundland on December 24! Who ever heard of such a thing? The butterfly seemed to be at home there, and fluttered from place to place, and then rested on the back of my mom's chair at the table, the one she would usually sit in, so my mom sat in the next chair. Then the butterfly left the back of the chair and actually rested right on the seat.

What happened next is absolutely amazing. The butterfly flew back up on the railings on the back of the chair, which is a dark brown colour, and, while she watched, the butterfly changed colour, from brown and blue to pure white!

My mom had tears in her eyes, and a voice thick with emotion, as she relayed this to us on Christmas Eve, while showing us the many pictures. She knew, just knew, it was Zachary, paying her a visit on Christmas Eve, letting us all know that he is okay, that he is always with us, which was the best Christmas gift we ever received!

The next two stories are connected. They are both written by relatives of Florence Pelley. The first comes from Florence's daughter-in-law, Sandra. The second was written by Florence's daughter Joyce. Butterflies certainly are important in their remembrance of Florence, and her husband, Harry, who passed away many years before her.

Flight of Fancy

SANDRA PELLEY

There is one person in our lives who is very special and whom we know is always there for us—our mom. I guess we all think Mom will be there forever, because she always has been. But there comes a time when she's not there anymore.

In July 2004, at the age of ninety-four, Florence Pelley, a mother of eight children, passed away. After we had the first viewing at the funeral home, with her lying there so peacefully, all of the family went back to the house. The "bridge," as she called it, was my favourite place to sit, because I liked the way that the sun was always shining there. As I sat, a butterfly came by. It circled around, touching each chair, and finally settling on Mom's chair. It flew around again a few times, continuing to land on the chairs, and then flew away.

As the family members came out to the bridge, I told them about the butterfly. Over the next couple of days, everyone saw it as it circled around. In one of the visits, it did its usual circle of the bridge and, as it finished, another butterfly flew in to accompany the first and they both flew off together.

One of Florence's sons, Reg, was unable to make it home for the funeral, but did arrive the next day. He and I were sitting on the bridge talking when the butterfly flew in. It flew in front of Reg and perched on the floor in front of him. The butterfly flapped its wings many times, then laid the wings flat and lay motionless for a second. Then the second butterfly flew in and they flew off together. My theory is that Mrs. Pelley had joined her husband, Harry, who died over thirty years ago, and he was accompanying her to the peaceful world he has lived in for all those years. He was waiting until it was time for her to join him.

Florence's daughter Joyce was left the task of closing the family home and distributing mementoes to various people. Just before she left to return to her home in British Columbia, realizing that she had packed all of her shirts, she went out to purchase a new one. The first store she went to, and the first T-shirt she saw, had a cluster of eight butterflies on the right-hand side of the shirt and one butterfly in the top left, in a flying-away motion. As mentioned earlier, Mrs. Pelley had eight children. Even more remarkable was the saying on the shirt, which said "Flight of Fancy." Mrs. Pelley's maiden name was Fancey. Joyce was stunned and, since the butterfly had become a special symbol to her, she immediately purchased the shirt.

I think Mrs. Pelley kept watch over her family during the three days after her death, coming to visit in spirit many times as the brightly coloured butterfly, a beautiful symbol of life, beauty, and peace. Is there any better symbol for a mom than a butterfly?

Just the Right Time

JOYCE DEERING

Cache Creek, British Columbia

Glenys and Paul Thorne have been great neighbours to our mom, always there for her in her deepest times of need. Glenys spent a great deal of time at the hospital with her during her last days on earth. She had been a nurse there. My brother Lon always calls Glenys his "angel," and I would have to agree with him!

When I was telling Glenys about Sandra's butterflies, she said, "Just a minute, I have a story for you." She told me, "On Wednesday I took the day off because I was so upset over losing my best friend. That day I took my three boys on an outing to the river, where they could swim and just be boys. They were also upset over Mrs. Pelley's death. While we were there, two butterflies kept flying around me. At one point one of the boys said, 'Look, Mommy, the butterflies are sitting on your shoulder.' I thought that that was very strange, but wonderful at the same time."

In a recent conversation with my brother Lon and his wife, Christine, they told me that a lone butterfly hung around their property far into the fall. When it started getting really cold, it huddled into the outside corner of the windowsill. Then one day, Christine told me she found the butterfly in her car and she took it out and put it in the shed. Just before Christmas, Lon

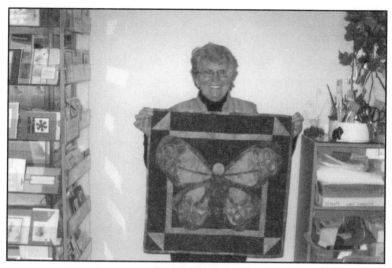

JOYCE DEERING

lit a fire in the workshop section of the shed. He then came back into the house until the shed warmed up. Lo and behold, on his return to the shed, there was the butterfly.

Recently in the area of Central Newfoundland, where Lon and Christine live, there was about four feet of snow on the ground. Christine told me that, one day when she opened the door, there was the butterfly, sitting on a snowbank.

When we returned to British Columbia, we decided we were going to go for a walk every day. Amazingly, on every single walk we were always accompanied by two butterflies. As the weather got colder, they disappeared, but I have no doubt they will be back in the spring. I can hardly wait! Since I returned home I have received numerous cards and gifts, always featuring butterflies. The strangest thing is that most of the people didn't know about the visits from the butterflies.

When I told the butterfly story to my family, they were in awe. One granddaughter was so taken up with it that everything she buys now must have a butterfly on it. She says that it keeps her close to her great-grandmother.

Now, I have to say that I do not believe that my mother was transformed into a butterfly. I do believe, however, that God puts these butterflies there at just the right time and makes us totally aware of them, and this helps the sadness leave us. Every time we see a beautiful butterfly, there is no question we will think of our mom.

The First Butterfly
of the Summer

ELSIE WATSON

Markham, Ontario

My sister, Jennie, who was nine years older than me, passed away with cancer at the age of seventy-eight. A week or so after my sister passed, I was down in the garden at our summer home on the Otterbury Road in Bareneed, pulling out wildflowers that had overgrown the winding path leading to the lower patio. I was thinking about my sister and was hoping to see a butterfly. I had heard about butterflies being messengers on a radio program earlier in the summer. I looked up and saw a very beautiful brown and orange butterfly, similar to a Monarch, sitting on a flower. I felt this butterfly was sent from Jennie, as it was the first butterfly I had seen all summer. I immediately went to get my camera, wondering if the butterfly would still be there when I got back, as I had to walk up the path quite a distance, cross the lawn and go into the house, and then go back down again. Just as I crossed the lawn and started to walk back down the path, the butterfly flew up directly toward me and landed on a daisy very close by. I got a beautiful photo. I believe Jennie sent the butterfly to me to let me know that she is as free as a butterfly now.

During a telephone conversation, I related this tale to a friend in Markham, Ontario, where I live when I am not in Newfoundland. She said the story gave her goosebumps, and she recounted that after her mother passed away, she was in the cemetery and a brightly coloured butterfly alighted on her mother's casket! She said this was most unexpected, as her mother passed away in November! She added that her mother had always loved bright colours.

That Sense of Peace

DARLENE WILTON

Woody Point, Newfoundland

I lost my son tragically in May as a result of a car acci-dent. Each day following Michael's funeral I visited his gravesite, and each day I would see the same butterfly floating all around me. I really believe my son wanted me to know that he was okay, and the butterfly always seemed to give me new hope and a sense of peace.

I had another experience in late October. I was sit-ting at my computer, as I've done many times before, just looking at pictures of my son. I was having a very rough day, and as I looked through the pictures, I had an overwhelming feeling of grief and sadness. I cried uncontrollably for what seemed like forever. Then, out of the corner of my eye, I thought I saw someone com-ing to my front door. When I looked up, there was a beautiful butterfly flying back and forth across my win-dow, its wings touching the windowpane. I was amazed and just watched it until it finally flew away. By this time I felt so much better, and that sense of peace had returned again.

I really believe there's something special about butterflies that none of us really understands. It is so nice to have the chance to share our experiences with others.

Now I Have Become A Believer

LEONA STROUD

Glovertown, Newfoundland

My sister Madeline had a granddaughter, Aliyah, who was born totally deaf. This broke Madeline's heart, and she would often call me and cry about it on the telephone. Sadly, Madeline died of a brain tumour on October 4, 2004, when she was only fifty-four years old.

As time went by, Aliyah was surgically implanted with a cochlear hearing aid, which allowed her to hear, and she has thrived ever since.

Approximately one year after my sister's death, my family was gathered together at a place called Drovers in Gambo. We were all there for a family cookout. My mom and I were sitting together on the beach and Aliyah was playing nearby. I said to my mom, "I wonder does Madeline know how well Aliyah is doing?" Mom replied, "I'm sure she does." At that moment, a big yellow butterfly appeared and landed on Aliyah's foot. The butterfly stayed there for a little while and then came and hovered over Mom and me. When we got up to leave, the butterfly followed us to our truck, and when we got into the truck the butterfly flew up into the sky.

I had heard stories of Butterfly Messengers before, but now I have become a believer.

"They're Still Here, Eric Boy"

DAN NORMAN

Gambo, Newfoundland

My brother Eric, with whom I was very close, died in 2006. Back in the early seventies, he and I had worked very hard to construct a log cabin at a small pond near Gambo. We spent many enjoyable days and nights there. At the pond we had our own special places to fish for trout. In May of this year, I decided to take an afternoon off and go there, as I always feel close to him when I visit our old haunt. I eventually wound up at Eric's favourite spot on the property. The evening was perfect, with the sun setting, the pond like a mirror, with a few flies alighting here and there. I began to think about Eric and how he would love to be there, especially after I hooked a nice-sized beauty. I said aloud, "They're still here, Eric boy."

Shortly after my comment, the first big Swallowtail Butterfly that I had seen for the year fluttered out of the woods, circled in front of the tip of my rod and flew back in the woods. Immediately a thought ran through my mind that it was Eric trying to tell me something. I felt that he was telling me, "Sure, I can do this anytime I want!" I know that he can, too!

I believe that there is only a fine line between life and those that have already passed on. I, for one, will not be afraid to go when my time comes.

And I Wonder

JOHN SHORTALL

St. John's, Newfoundland

I have always thought that there was something to the stories of people having an experience with a butterfly after someone near to them has died, but when I mentioned it to others they told me I was crazy. I still believe, and here is my story.

My wife died in June of 1995, and during her wake, my cousin showed up at our house with a flower for the family. Instead of bringing it to the funeral home, I kept it at my house, with the intention of eventually putting it on my wife's grave. However, I thought it over and instead chose to put it in our back garden.

Time went by, winter came, and the following spring I was out in the garden on a cool June day, too cool and too early in the year for butterflies, when a black and orange butterfly came over the fence and started flying around the garden. Needless to say, I was surprised to see it because of the kind of day it was. I remember saying to myself, "If you land on the flower given to me by my cousin, it will certainly be a sign." Well, out of all of the flowers in the garden, the butterfly landed on the flower given to me in my wife's memory. It stayed there while I went and got my camera and took a picture of it, which I still have.

You can decide for yourself what the butterfly symbolizes. I have no explanation for it being there that day. But every now and then, I see another black and orange butterfly and I wonder . . .

"Hi, This Is Niki"

PAMELA MARTIN

Gambo, Newfoundland

I have always been a believer in life after death. It is so much more beautiful and a lot less scary to think of death as a beginning rather than an end, and that it is possible that we may return to the earth as something beautiful and inspirational. It is especially moving when your beliefs are confirmed in ways that could never be chance or mere coincidence, but can only be explained as a direct message from someone whom you have deeply loved and lost. Such is the case of my best friend, Niki, who died on August 21, 2002, at the age of twenty.

In early 2002, while she and I were enrolled in our second year of university, Niki became ill. I remember nights when she would cry out in her sleep and awaken terrified after experiencing horrible nightmares. After months of mysterious eye troubles and strange muscle weakness, she was diagnosed with terminal brain cancer. The doctor explained that it was called pontine brainstem glioma, a rare form of diffuse cancerous tumour for which there was no cure. To make matters worse, it was a very aggressive form of cancer, and even with treatment she would probably only have another year to live. I remember feeling chilled to the bone when she told me the news. I stayed with her in hospital as often as I could until she was allowed to go home, and I was so amazed by how positive she was. Even after receiving such horrible news, she was just thankful that she had her friends and family by her side.

Over the next few months, despite the fact that Niki was undergoing radiation treatment and taking countless medications, her condition rapidly deteriorated. She was always such a free spirit who loved life and enjoyed every day that she was alive, and now it was all slipping away. I remember having to hide my tears one day as I watched her desperately trying to hold a pencil, when just a few days before she could write with ease. Her eyesight deteriorated, her hair began to fall out and she was gradually losing the ability to walk. It was as though an invisible thief was stealing my best friend's life away a little piece at a time and there was nothing I could do to stop it.

I spent countless hours researching her condition on the Internet, looking for new forms of cancer treatment, emailing oncologists in different countries, trying in vain to find anything that might provide even the faintest glimmer of hope for a cure, but I found nothing. I did, however, manage to find a wish foundation that was willing to grant her wish of going on a cruise with her mom, which she did that summer.

As part of the whole process of acceptance, we talked openly about death and even laughed about it sometimes. One day she told me that she had decided to stop her medications and radiation therapy because they were making her so sick. She also asked me what I thought would happen to her spirit after she was gone. I said that I believe that we are never truly gone when we die, but rather our souls come back to the earth as something beautiful. Niki had always loved butterflies and had collected many butterfly trinkets throughout her life. She even had a butterfly tattoo that she was particularly proud of. She said that if she were to choose, she would come back as a butterfly because they were symbolic of new life. I told her that if I was right and that there was a life after death, she had to promise to reach me and show me a sign that she was with me . . . and she did.

In August of 2002, Niki became too sick to remain at home any longer and was admitted to the palliative care unit. I knew it would only be a matter of days before she would be gone. She was unable to swallow or speak and was blind, but I knew she could hear me because she would squeeze my hand whenever she heard my voice. She eventually slipped into a coma. Early in the morning of August 22, after returning home from another day at the hospital, I received a phone call that she was gone. I felt relief and sadness all at once, for I knew that I would miss my dearest friend but was grateful that her suffering was finally over. Since Niki's death, I had come to learn that the love of a friend can bridge any gap, even between life and death itself.

Two days later, during her funeral, I remember feeling as though I would never be able to get past the loss of such an important part of my life and that nobody could ever take her place. After it was over, I was the first to leave the service because I just wanted to get away from it all. My eyes welled up with tears that I had tried so desperately to hold back throughout the service, and as I ran to the end of the parking lot I cried so hard that I could barely catch my breath. It was then that I saw something that made me stop dead in my tracks. A beautiful Monarch Butterfly, bigger than any I have ever seen before, fluttered toward me, bouncing on the air. I laughed and cried at the same time as it danced all around me in circles. I reached out my hand to touch it and it flew around my hands, weaving through my fingers. It finally came to rest on my shoulder for a moment, and I closed my eyes and felt the warmth of the sun. With that, it flew away, touching its velvet wings to my face as it left.

AIMEE NICOLE "NIKI" FORTIER

One thing that I kept as a reminder of Niki after she was gone was a message from her that she had left on my answering service. Every time I checked my messages I was prompted to delete it, but I never could bring myself to do it. Exactly one year after her death, I was having a quiet morning moment on my back patio, when a beautiful butterfly, a huge yellow and black one this time, came and flew around and around where I was sitting.

"Hi Niki," I said as it landed on my finger for a few seconds and flew off over the roof of my house. I felt an incredible warmth inside because I just knew it was her.

The telephone rang and I went inside. As I picked up the phone I heard on the other line, "Hi, this is Niki. I just wanted to say hello and tell you I can't wait to see you today . . ."

It was her message from over a year before that I had been keeping for so long. To this day I will never understand how the message came to play back in such a way, but I don't even need to question why it did.

In 2004 I became pregnant with my first child, but miscarried at just under four months. I had numerous complications and lost so much blood that I began to go into shock. I remember little about the incident, as I slipped in and out of consciousness. However, I do have a memory of the most beautiful dream. In it I could see Niki surrounded by warm light and millions of butterflies. There were so many that all I could hear was the sound of beating wings, and she told me to fight because it wasn't my time. I felt her with me throughout the whole thing and it helped me make it through. I have since been blessed with a healthy baby boy who is now four years old.

On my last day of nursing school, my class gathered for a farewell meal, and a butterfly decided to make an appearance in the school cafeteria. It landed on my table, crawled onto my hand, and I brought it outside. I have seen butterflies in the dead of winter appearing out of nowhere in the falling snow. I have seen them at night as I stand on my deck, looking at the moon on a sleepless night. I see them if I'm perhaps driving a little too fast, and they seem to remind me to slow down and be careful.

I could write a pretty amazing list of all of the significant times that I have seen butterflies, but there are so many. To me, their existence is a constant reminder that we never truly leave this world when we die. They also remind me of just how powerful love can be. Niki watches over me; I know this without a doubt because of the butterflies I see as the fulfillment of her promise. I believe that when we have lost someone we love, there are always signs to show us that they are still with us . . . it's just up to us to see them and to believe.

I have included this final story for several reasons. I wanted to show that butterflies are not the only symbols our loved ones use to communicate with us after they have gone. I have heard messenger stories about animals, as well as many about birds. This next story falls into the latter category, and the birds in the story could not have been more appropriate, based on the life of the person involved.

Gerard Leonard was a friend of mine and, like me, he was a great admirer of Irish and folk music. He also loved the outdoors and nature, and worked most of his career with the Provincial Forestry Department. During the latter part of his career, after the Forestry and Wildlife departments were merged into one, he became involved with bird studies, especially those involved with Willow and Rock Ptarmigan. These birds are usually referred to as Partridge in Newfoundland. This story was written by Gerard's close friend and co-worker, Bill Greene.

The Partridge

BILL GREENE
Pasadena, Newfoundland

On November 23, 2009, my closest and lifelong friend passed away suddenly, struck down by a massive heart attack. Although Gerard had not been feeling well for several weeks, his passing came as a great shock to his family, friends, and co-workers.

One of Gerard's daughters, Mara, was travelling in Thailand at the time of her father's death. When she got the devastating news about her father, she had to start a three-day journey to make it back to Newfoundland for his funeral. She was sitting on a bench in Bangkok Airport waiting for her flight and desperately trying to telephone home to her mother on her cellphone. The battery in her phone had run out and she was sitting there, steeped in grief because of her father's passing, and upset about not being able to call home. A gentleman sitting beside her saw her plight and asked her what was wrong. She told him the story of her dad dying and how she was trying to phone home to comfort her mother and two sisters, and how her cellphone had run out of power. Immediately he gave Mara his phone to use and asked if she would mind if he prayed for her father. When he started to pray, a small bird appeared, flew all around Mara, and landed by her feet. It walked around for a few seconds and then flew away. Her father, Gerard, had always loved songbirds, and this was certainly a great comfort to Mara, being so far from home and going through such grief.

Gerard was from Placentia, on the east coast of Newfoundland. His brothers and sisters still lived in that area, and they made the long journey across the island together to attend the wake at Marble Mountain on the west coast. They were passing by Gambo in Central Newfoundland, when a car several vehicles ahead of them hit a partridge as it flew across the road. The impact with the car caused feathers from the bird to fly up in the air and back toward their vehicle. One of the feathers hooked in the radio antenna, and it stayed there for the entire drive to Corner Brook, a distance of about 400 kilometres.

Gerard's brother Tom had told me this story while I was attending the wake. He took me out to the parking lot and showed me the feather still clinging to the antenna. He took it off and put it in an envelope. He said he was going to bring it back to Placentia to give to his mother, who was too frail to make the trip across the island. There could not have been a better sign from Gerard than to have a partridge feather cling to their vehicle, on a journey to see him for the last time.

Author's Note

The stories in this book are just a small sampling of the many that I believe are out there. I suspect that, after publication of this book, many other "Butterfly Messenger" stories will begin to emerge. I would like to encourage any of you who have had an experience similar to the people in this book to record your experience, and to encourage any family members and friends to do the same with their stories as well. I hope there will be a second edition of *Butterfly Messengers*, with even more stories of comfort and hope.

Please send your stories to me by email at lloydh@nf.sympatico.ca, or you can get them to me the old-fashioned way by sending them by post to:

Lloyd Hollett
17 King Street
Pasadena, NL
A0L 1K0 Canada

No story is too long or too short. The more detail you put in your story, the more interesting it is for the reader. I would like to include your name and your hometown, but if you do not feel comfortable doing this, you are under no obligation. My only request is that the story be your own experience or one told to you by a close relative or friend.

Acknowledgements

I would like to thank everyone who shared their stories with me. Without you this book would not have been possible. The process of gathering and reading all your stories has been a wonderful journey for me, and a journey that I have to say became very much a spiritual one. It has been an honour to meet you through your stories and play a small part of your message of comfort and hope.

I would like to thank Garry and Margo Cranford for their encouragement and guidance. Thank you to the people at Flanker Press for your attention to detail and your determination to make the book the special project that it is.

My thanks to all my family and friends who supported my efforts and encouraged me to pursue this project. A special thank you to Guy Romaine for his mastery of the English language by proofing the manuscript and for the helpful advice in the organization of the stories.

A special thank you to my family. To my sons, Matthew and Adam, for showing your interest and encouraging me along the way. To my daughter, Kelly, for all your help with the editing, proofreading, and checking my punctuation skills!

Finally to my wife, Sandy, for putting up with all the late nights, messy kitchen table, and missed games of cards for the past two years. Thanks for cooking supper as "silently as possible" while I worked and for those little "shopping trips" so I could have some quiet time. I couldn't have done this without your love, support, and encouragement.

Index

LLOYD HOLLETT was born in Harbour Buffett, Placentia Bay, and at the age of two moved to the community of Little Harbour East. He attended high school in the nearby town of Arnold's Cove. After graduating from college with a diploma in Forest Resources Technology in 1977, he started working in St. John's with the provincial Department of Forestry as a Protection Technician. In 1984 when the provincial forestry department was relocated to Corner Brook, he moved with his family to Pasadena in western Newfoundland.

In 1998 Lloyd co-founded the Newfoundland Insectarium, where he is the owner and director. In addition to operating the Insectarium he travels extensively throughout Eastern Canada giving school presentations.

More recently, his love of Irish and folk music has prompted him to establish Front Row Promotions, organizing performances across Newfoundland for international recording artists.

He is married to the former Sandy Frampton and they have three children, Matthew, Kelly and Adam.

Butterfly Messengers is his first book.